LUIS PALAU

with **JAY FORDICE**

D0974157

CHANGED
BY FAITH

Dare to Trust God with Your Broken Pieces . . .
and Watch What Happens

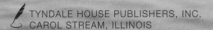

TYNDALE HOUSE PUBLISHERS, INC.
CAROL STREAM, ILLINOIS

Visit Tyndale's exciting Web site at www.tyndale.com.

TYNDALE and Tyndale's quill logo are registered trademarks of Tyndale House Publishers, Inc.

Changed by Faith: Dare to Trust God with Your Broken Pieces . . . and Watch What Happens

Cover concept by Katie Bredemeier

Designed by Beth Sparkman

Library of Congress Cataloging-in-Publication Data

Palau, Luis, date.
   Changed by faith : dare to trust God with your broken pieces . . . and watch what happens / Luis Palau with Jay Fordice.
     p. cm.
   Includes bibliographical references.
   ISBN 978-1-4143-3622-0 (sc)
   1. Trust in God—Christianity. 2. Providence and government of God. 3. Consolation. 4. Christian life. I. Fordice, Jay. II. Title. III. Title: Dare to trust God with your broken pieces . . . and watch what happens.
   BT135.P38 2011
   248—dc22   2010036519

Printed in the United States of America

17 16 15 14 13 12 11
7   6   5   4   3   2   1

To my four godly daughters-in-law:

Michelle Morford Palau,
Gloria Holden Palau,
Wendy Levy Palau, and
Megan Cochran Palau.

Contents

Introduction

I HAVE A FRIEND who is struggling through her eleventh bout with cancer. Ever since she was nineteen years old, it has been an ongoing battle. Cervical cancer. Uterine cancer. Ovarian cancer. Thyroid cancer. Lymph cancer. Stomach cancer. Breast cancer—twice. Malignant melanomas—twice. And now—colon cancer, stage three. Every time, she has beaten it. Every time, she has come out on top. But it hasn't been easy. In fact, it has been downright excruciating at times. It has worn her down and left her weak.

But that's not the whole story.

Over her thirty-five years of trials and testing, my friend has stood strong. With tears at times. In pain nearly constantly. But she stands, to this day, a beautiful example of strength and power. And what many would expect would leave her discouraged and deflated has only succeeded in strengthening her faith.

In reality, we all face hardships. Not everyone will be tested as severely as my friend has been, but there's no question that life can get tough. Trials will come. Expectations will be crushed. Dreams may be dashed. Whether our challenges are big or small, we all deal with our fair share of trials and disappointments in life. And if we're not careful, they will cause us to crash.

I know. I've been there.

For me, the crash came when I was thirty-five years old.

◫   ◫   ◫

From the time my wife, Patricia, and I first met—in Portland, Oregon, in 1960—we both had our sights set on the mission field, working to share the Good News of Jesus Christ with people around the world. After we finished our biblical training in 1961, we immediately set out on our adventure, wasting no time. Married a few short months after graduation and soon thereafter commissioned by OC International, we moved to Detroit for an intensive seven-month training course called M.I. (Missionary Internship).

From Detroit, we were sent to Costa Rica. From Costa Rica, we went to Colombia. And from Colombia to Mexico.

From our new base in Mexico, Patricia and I and a small team of missionaries began preparing for evangelistic campaigns all over Latin America. With a vision to proclaim the Good News to entire regions, we dreamed big and envisioned great success. We held major evangelistic festivals throughout Central and South America, partnering with hundreds of churches and reaching thousands of individuals. In some countries, we found great open doors. In others, great opposition. It was tough. We were exhausted. But there was purpose in it. And we felt fulfilled . . . until the summer of 1969.

For more than six months, our small team had been planning a major initiative in a key Latin American city. We had rented out a local baseball stadium, enlisted support from thousands of volunteers, and paid for extensive publicity. Our goal was to hold a two-week campaign—to share the message of Jesus with as many people as possible in the most public way. I had spent many sleepless nights preparing for the event, which was the biggest I had planned thus far in my career. I had poured my blood, sweat, and tears into the project. And now, only days away, with our advertisements plastered across the city, you could sense the excitement on our team and among the partnering churches. We were sure God was preparing to do something big—to use us in powerful ways.

Our entire team was engaged with the campaign. We had dreamed of something like this for years and had been working overtime for several months to roll it out. To finally see it coming to fruition was overwhelming, to say the least.

Under the surface, however, all was not well. The truth was, we had gone out on a limb financially preparing for the event. I called it faith, but it really wasn't. Instead of having the peace that accompanies true faith in God, I was antsy and impatient. In a rush to move forward with my vision for the event, I unwisely borrowed money from friends and churches, fully believing that the money raised through offerings during the two weeks would cover the costs. But it never occurred to me that the event might never happen.

Little did I know that the government would revoke our permit two days before opening night.

I received the call from one of my team members.

"Luis," he said in a panic, "they shut us down. They pulled the plug."

"What are you talking about?" I said. "What do you mean, they shut us down?"

"The authorities. The government. They pulled our permit. It's over. We're done. They said, 'You cannot have your campaign. It's against our laws . . . and you are foreigners. And if we catch you trying, you're going to jail.'"

That was it. The permit was revoked. Our campaign was over before it started. With no avenue for appeal, our six months of planning went up in smoke.

I immediately felt sick. After hours on the phone with city leaders—anyone I could complain to or ask for answers—I finally gave up in despair. All that work. All that preparation. All for naught.

The blow nearly did me in . . . literally. I ended up in bed with a fever but no real illness. For three weeks, I lay in my room, with no desire to get up, no motivation to start again. I was defeated, exhausted, and just plain spent. In the midst of wanting to offer hope to others, I had lost it myself. We now had bills to pay and no revenue. We had apology notes to write. We had our mission and our friends to answer to. The questions would be endless.

I couldn't stop my mind from spinning with thoughts.

Why the change of mind? Why this? Why now? Why me? Why here?

My mind raced and my body ached. Eventually, I found the strength to pray.

"Lord, I believe. I really do. But what good is it? What are you doing? And why do you seem so far away?"

My faith was shaken and my convictions were under attack. Did I really believe what I said I believed? Was this all worth it, even in the pain? I had gone through the motions. I had done the right things. I had trusted the Lord—*I really had!* So why wasn't life turning out the way I expected?

Throughout this time, Patricia was amazing. She cared for me, but she challenged me as well. I remember her saying, "Luis, what are you doing in bed? Get up. Keep going! This isn't the end of you."

During those three weeks, God was working powerfully in my life. He stripped me of myself, realigned my priorities, and reminded me of the basic, foundational truths of my faith. It was painful, but it was powerful.

As he worked me over, there was only one thing I could bring myself to do. I read like a madman—mainly the Bible. "If this book is true . . . if it really is what I say it is," I told myself, "it must have answers." And I was determined to find them. I was determined to scour its pages until I found them.

I focused my attention on the Gospel of John. I read it in every translation in every language I could understand. And as I pored over the pages, I was deeply transformed. I found my priorities being realigned, my perspective changing, and my understanding of God—my Lord—adapting into something far more powerful . . . far more profound.

Those three weeks of searching changed me completely. And though it was painful, it proved to be the beginning of great things—not the end of my ministry, as I had feared. But it was only after I had done my own soul-searching and my own searching for God, only after I had come to terms with the true Savior—not the one I had created to fit in my own little box—that I could deal with the realities of life and move on to greater things.

Eventually, we held an evangelistic campaign in that city. It was far different than we had ever dreamed, and it was done in the Lord's timing. He used it in powerful ways—in our own lives and in the lives of the people we reached. He moved us to different locations, bringing friends and partners alongside to fill the gaps in our funding and offset our financial shortfalls. All our bills were paid. All debt was forgiven. And just as he has done with so many others throughout history, Jesus showed up just at the right time and dealt with my unbelief.

Since that pivotal summer more than forty years ago, my life and ministry have been radically different. God has done powerful things through me and my entire family—not because of us (in fact, in many ways in spite of us), but because he cares for us and wants to work through us.

Reflecting recently on how Patricia and I have been used in ministry over the years, I was amazed and humbled. God has taken us to more than seventy nations and has allowed us to present a clear case for Jesus to more than one billion people through television, radio, print, and live events. He has allowed me to speak face-to-face with more than twenty-eight million people, has allowed our team to partner with tens of thousands of churches, and has allowed me to speak directly to presidents, royalty, and other leaders throughout the world. Best of all, he has allowed me to lead tens of thousands of individuals—if not more—to a personal commitment to Jesus Christ.

Looking back, I realize that the summer of 1969 was a defining moment for me. I wouldn't be where I am today if I hadn't gone through that season of testing. The questions I asked were healthy ones. The pain was necessary. It stripped away the façade and established who I really was and who I was really serving. Ultimately, it bolstered my faith and showed me the true power of the gospel.

I'm sure you've dealt with something similar. The promotion you worked so hard to attain yet never received. The business venture you risked your life savings on, only to lose every last bit of it. The boyfriend or girlfriend, husband or wife, for whom you put your life on the line, only to be left empty-handed and broken. The children you worked so hard to raise, only to be left disappointed and in pain. The family you loved, only to be rejected. The house you mortgaged—and lost to foreclosure.

Sure, you continue in your faith. You still believe what you believe. But there are questions. Deep questions. The pain lingers. And the transformed life promised by preachers like me seems to be just as far away as when you began the journey.

We've all felt it—the rejection, the confusion, the devastation, the lack of answers. It's almost a rite of passage. But is there real, life-changing hope in the midst of it all? I believe there is. I'd like to tell you that your best days could very well still be ahead of you—if you trust God.

But how do you get there?

How do you overcome your current situation?

How do you allow yourself to be changed by faith?

Those are the deep questions. Those are the tough questions. And those are exactly the questions I hope to help you answer for yourself.

1

EXPECT MORE

THE CONVERTIBLE LAY upside down in pieces across the rain-soaked motorway just outside London. Tire tread, debris, and scraped pavement trailed behind the car for more than forty feet. Steam hissed from the smashed engine. Metal crunched and glass cracked as the small car rocked back and forth on its hood.

Grant, the nineteen-year-old driver, had been thrown from the wreckage, sent flying over the side barrier upon impact. He lay limp and unconscious in the bushes beside the road. Though he was bruised and battered, his wounds would not prove fatal. Brandy—his passenger and girlfriend—was not as fortunate. Held tightly in her seat by the belt across her lap, she had been flipped and flung as the vehicle cartwheeled across the road. She was dead before the car came to a stop.

It was three days before her sixteenth birthday.

I received the news just a few hours after the accident— awakened by the telephone in the early morning hours. I rubbed my eyes and reached for the phone. It was my good friend Bill, Grant's father, and I could tell he was shaken up.

"Luis, it's awful," he began.

"Bill, what's going on? What happened?"

"Grant and Brandy—they were in an accident. You remember Brandy, right?"

"Of course I remember Brandy. How is she? How are they? Tell me, what happened?"

Bill hesitated. I could tell he was fighting back tears. "It's not good, Luis. Grant is in hospital. But Brandy . . . Brandy is gone."

"What happened?"

"Luis, it was stupid. The two were out for a drive—just heading to the store. Grant was driving too fast through the hills in the rain, and he lost control of the car. One split second."

"Bill, I'm so sorry. What can I do?"

"Come. Come to England. We need you here. Brandy's family needs you. Her mother asked for you specifically."

I was quiet, still trying to absorb the news.

"Come do the memorial service, will you?" he insisted. "You played such a significant role in Brandy's life. I know it's what she would want."

"Of course I'll come, Bill."

I was on a plane to London's Heathrow Airport before the week was out.

❖   ❖   ❖

As I sat in the airplane, jet engines humming in the background, I couldn't help but think back to the first time I met young Brandy. It was three years earlier, at a youth gathering where I was scheduled to speak. She had come with her new boyfriend, Grant, and she was beaming from ear to ear. Little did I know that her smile masked a world of pain.

To all appearances, Brandy had everything going for her. She was bright and beautiful and came from a well-to-do family. Her father was a classical musician, and her mother was a television personality. And now she had a handsome boyfriend from a good family as well. Her future looked bright. I would later come to find out that her life was nowhere near as perfect as she let on.

As I shared my message that day, challenging the crowd to give their lives to Jesus Christ and to let him take their ashes and turn them into something beautiful, I had a sense I was speaking directly to Brandy. Sure enough, at the end of my talk, when I gave the invitation, she was among the first to stand and make her way to the stage—running, not walking, with Grant following quickly behind.

I jumped off the stage and found Brandy in the crowd. I could see she wanted to talk, and I wanted to offer her encouragement and guidance. As we sat down together, along with Grant, I asked her questions about her life, knowing that my message had struck a chord. Now, even three years later, her story was still fresh in my mind.

"Brandy, what's on your heart?" I asked.

"I need help."

"What do you mean?"

"My life—it's just not what I would have ever dreamed it would be."

"Tell me."

"I feel so alone. I feel unloved. My parents don't get along, and they're too busy for me. I don't even live with them. No one seems to care."

I could sense the pain hiding just below the surface.

"Why don't you live with your parents?"

"They divorced several years ago and live in different areas. I'm just a distraction to them. They sent me to live with my aunt and uncle, so I only see them on occasion. I feel tossed around—and that's just the beginning. Why is life so difficult?"

"Brandy, I'm sorry," I said. "Sometimes that's just the way it is. But you're wrong about no one caring. There *is* someone who cares. There *is* a reason for hope. You were made for more than this."

I could tell she was still processing my message, but it was beginning to click in her mind.

"Do you go to church, Brandy?"

"No. My parents have never been into religion. And my aunt and uncle are atheists."

"Have you ever read the Bible?"

"No. Never."

"So, what do you believe?"

"I don't really know. But your message—it made sense."

"Brandy, there is someone who cares about you. There is someone who wants to see you succeed. He wants to give you purpose, joy, and a truly meaningful life. His name is Jesus."

"I'm just not sure," she said.

"I know. The world is full of trouble. Your life isn't perfect. You have struggles. You have pain. But Jesus came to overcome the trouble and pain of this world. He came to give you life!"

Over the next several minutes, Brandy continued to pour out her pain and her struggles as Grant and I tried to encourage her. She was so lonely, so broken, so discouraged. She wanted hope. She needed a fresh start. She craved something or someone she could trust. Her parents had let her down. Her aunt and uncle, though they had opened their home to her, were not always there for her emotionally. There were so many insecurities, so many painful memories, and so many unanswered questions. And she was still so young.

Finally, I knew it was time to challenge her. Looking her straight in the eye, I said, "Brandy, do you want your life to change? Do you want to see success where there is failure now? Do you want real, transforming purpose in your life?"

"I want it more than anything in the world," she said, now on the verge of tears.

"So tell me, Brandy, why did you come forward?"

"Because I want to know Jesus!"

As we continued to talk, I was amazed by her humility, hunger, and eagerness to learn. You could tell the message had shaken her. And as I explained in more detail what it meant to follow Jesus as her Savior, she understood perfectly. She got it. That day, Brandy gave her life over to Jesus and became a new creation.

Over the next three years, Brandy's life was radically transformed. Even as a young teenager, she saw God do powerful things. She became a winsome encourager among her friends, and her life exuded purpose, hope, and joy. She couldn't stop talking about Jesus, and she couldn't keep from smiling.

Even her parents saw something captivating in Brandy. As she spent more time with her mother and father and their high-society friends, they were all encouraged and blessed by her. People were drawn to Brandy, and she was always quick to tell them that the real attraction was Jesus. Even her aunt and uncle—both staunch atheists—eventually made their own commitment to Jesus Christ. They both admitted to me personally that it was a direct result of Brandy's life and testimony. Brandy's life had been powerfully transformed. There was no question about that.

◈   ◈   ◈

At the memorial service, the church was packed with musicians and movie stars, high school students, family members, friends, and acquaintances. As I stood in front of the casket and shared about Brandy's life, I was amazed at how in three short years this sweet, little girl had touched the lives of literally hundreds of people. Her life had gone from painful to powerful. She and everyone around her had seen her ashes turned to beauty. Her life and her story had been redeemed.

This young girl accomplished more in those three years than many people accomplish in a lifetime. And her story is a challenge to each one of us. Brandy was a baby in terms of her spiritual walk. But she was faithful. And she saw God use her in powerful ways.

Ashes into beauty. Pain into power. Rejection into rejoicing. It's something we all desire. And it's within our reach.

So why don't we see more of it?

Why don't we see more radical transformation in people's lives? In our own lives?

Why don't we experience a more thrilling adventure of faith and trust—just like Brandy?

To be honest, many of us have become comfortable Christians. We go to church; we believe that the Bible is true; we've been to Sunday school; and we have the right answers and can cite the right verses; but in many ways we have become lethargic, pew-sitting believers. Others have given up on church completely. Their fire has died down to embers, and they've resigned themselves to the conclusion that profound transformation—which the Bible seems to promise—is something they won't fully realize until they get to heaven. Though in the meantime they may experience some wisps and whispers of God's power, for the most part life is too cruel and their circumstances are too difficult to see that God is actively at work right here and right now.

❖ ❖ ❖

Maybe your problem is a crisis of belief. Maybe you feel as if your circumstances are so far out of control that only a complete miracle could make any difference.

Well, it's hard to imagine circumstances more out of control than the situations faced by many throughout the Bible. We read stories of sick women, blind beggars, guilt-ridden fathers, even murderers and prostitutes. We are reminded of God's power as he takes these individuals and transforms their lives into something beautiful. The Bible is full of stories of individuals in far worse situations than ours . . . people who called upon the name of the Lord and found healing, hope, encouragement, and new life.

One story that always strikes me with power is found three places in the Bible (Matthew 17:14-20; Mark 9:14-29; and Luke 9:1-6, 37-43). It's the story of a demon-possessed boy and a father who struggled with his faith.

If you're familiar with the story, you know that the boy had been afflicted since childhood with an evil spirit. The father had brought the boy to some of Jesus' disciples to see

if they could cast out the demon; but they were unable to—
even though Jesus had specifically given them the power and
authority to heal.

When Jesus eventually arrived on the scene, the father,
who by then was at the end of his rope, pleaded with Jesus
to heal his son. He called out to him, "Teacher, I brought my
son so you could heal him. . . . Have mercy on us and help
us, *if you can.*"[1]

"What do you mean, 'If I can'?" Jesus asked. "Anything is
possible if a person believes."[2]

As soon as the father realized his folly, he fell down next
to his son at Jesus' feet. With tears in his eyes and pain in his
voice, he humbly pleaded, "I do believe; *help my unbelief.*"[3]

At that, Jesus turned to the boy, knelt down, and prayed.
With authority and power he rebuked the evil spirit. And
within seconds, the boy was healed. Peace returned to his
young body. Hope returned to the scene.

❖　　❖　　❖

If you're at all like me, when you read a story like that, you
get encouraged. You get excited to see Jesus show up to save
the day and bring peace and wholeness back to the scene.
After all, it's what we all want. It's what we all dream of,
deep down. We breathe a sigh of relief when we see that God
truly cares about our circumstances and that he truly is able
to heal, even in the midst of our weak faith. And you can't

help but wonder if he will do the same for you . . . someday
. . . in some way.

But now for the hard questions: How often have you seen
a scenario like that played out in your own life? How often
have you really, truly seen Jesus show up and do something so
dramatic? Where was he when your friend died? Why did he
seem distant when your job disappeared? Why didn't he stop
the cancer? Where was his grace when your spouse decided
to leave? Why would he let you lose your baby?

It's not that you don't believe. Like Brandy, you trust that
Jesus is alive. Like the father of the young boy, you believe, at
least in part, that Jesus can have an impact on your life. You
know he's at work in the world. You believe in miracles—
you've just never actually seen one. You wonder why God
is so silent at times, and why you're not able to bring his
power to bear in your own family, community, or circumstances. Maybe, you tell yourself, Jesus just hasn't shown up
yet. Maybe his attention is focused someplace else—in Haiti
or India or somewhere in Africa. But in *your* life . . . with
your circumstances . . . you just don't see it. After all, does
Jesus really care about you? Does he really have the power
and desire to take your ashes—your pain—and turn them
into beauty?

Still, you'd like to believe that the same purpose and
power that Brandy experienced is available to you. In fact,
you do believe it's *possible*, but you want to experience it for
yourself—right now. Just like the father in the story, when

confronted with tough situations, you can't help but utter the words, *"Lord, I believe. Please help my unbelief."*

◈   ◈   ◈

On the other hand, maybe you've become a cynic. You believe that God exists and you have at least a vague understanding of Jesus. But you just don't buy into the hype about modern-day miracles and life transformation. And frankly, you don't see much difference between some Christians you know and anyone else. Sure, faith in Jesus may be great for others, but what's the point for you? Why should you really care? And why should you subject yourself to that sort of religious lifestyle? It's so confining—so restricting. Besides, is it really real?

Wherever you fall on the spectrum of faith, I'm sure you've thought to yourself on occasion, *What's the point?* You question whether faith in God—or trust in Jesus and his Word—can really make a difference in your daily life.

We all have times of questioning—wondering about the purpose of it all. We've all had our fair share of trials. We've felt the pain, struggled with the despair, and been left asking why. We get tired of the rat race and tired of this boring old life. In desperation, we call out to God. We ask Jesus to show up and bring peace and liberation to the scene—to transform our lives into something truly meaningful and powerful. And yet, he seems oddly silent. We're left wondering, *Jesus, where are you? Jesus, what am I missing?*

Apathy sets in. Despair takes over.

Like most of us, you shut yourself off from the rest of the world—while preserving the illusion of being connected—and continue life as best you can.

But you were made for more than that!

◉   ◉   ◉

We live in a broken world. But I don't have to tell you that. We've all had our lives come crashing down around us at one time or another. We've felt the weight on our shoulders, and we've crumbled under the pressure. Some have turned to alcohol, drugs, food, sex, or other pursuits in order to get through it. Others fantasize about suicide, winning the lottery, or finding their soul mate. It seems we'll turn to anything to find comfort. We're all looking to fill our lives with something. And yet the next morning, the pain is still there; the wounds are still fresh.

Let's face it: All too often, our lives are not what we hoped they would be. The grass is never green enough. The sky is never blue enough. The vacation is never sweet enough, long enough, or relaxing enough. The money never goes far enough. The relationships never satisfy. The expectations never pan out. And the plans never turn out the way we expected. Regardless of what we believe, we all seem to be struggling with the same not-quite-what-I-signed-up-for reality.

If that is where you find yourself today, take heart! No

matter what you're struggling with, there's hope. I know it! I've experienced it, and I want to share it with you. As you read this book and consider how this all fits together, I want to encourage you to think long and hard about who you really are, what life is really all about, what you really believe, and how God—our Creator—fits into your story, if at all. I'm not talking about a "Sunday only" type of faith. I'm talking about real, transformational faith. I'm talking about a life that is worth living—and a faith that doesn't disappoint. After all, isn't that what we all want?

I'm not writing just to make an argument. I'm writing from my heart, which is why you'll find elements of my own story throughout these pages. I'm writing from personal experience, from my deep passion for other people and for God, and from my desire to see people set free to live life the way it was meant to be lived.

Jesus is still alive. He is at work. He is redeeming our lives. And yes, just as he did for Brandy and the demon-possessed boy, he is still raising people from the ash heap of life.

It's time to stop holding your breath and expecting the worst. It's time to stop merely dreaming of a better life. Whether or not you can see where the road leads from where you're standing doesn't matter. It's time to put your faith in the one who sees the end from the beginning, the one who has the power to cast out demons, heal our diseases, and set our feet on solid ground.

It's time to say, "I believe. Lord, help my unbelief!"

2

KNOW THYSELF

SOMETIME DURING the second century, high in the hills of southern Greece, the famous Greek traveler and geographer Pausanias found himself standing at the foot of the Temple of Apollo, dwarfed and in awe. In all his travels throughout the land, this was the one structure that left him nearly speechless. Set as an imposing sentinel on the southern slope of the mountain of Parnassus, surrounded by the beauty of the city of Delphi, this was the temple written about from antiquity, dreamed about in literature, and immortalized in Greek mythology. Its sheer size puts the Parthenon to shame, and its precision still baffles architects today.

As Pausanias took in this magnificent sight, he found a

large boulder on which to sit, pulled out his notes, and began to document the structure—every feature, every nuance. His descriptions and observations would be studied for centuries to come.

The geographer took great pains to describe every detail. And as his eyes moved upward, his interest was captured by an inscription, clearly visible from where he sat below.

Towering overhead, etched into the marble, read the now-famous quote attributed to any number of Greek philosophers: *Gnothi Sauton.*

Know Thyself.

More than eighteen hundred years after Pausanias's travels, many of us have yet to meet the demands of that inscription. Many have struggled, and failed, to truly *know* themselves.

At some point, we all ask ourselves the same questions, in one form or another:

Who am I?
Where did I come from? Who made me?
Why am I here? What is my purpose in life?
Where am I going when I die?
What does it mean to live an excellent life?
Does any of this really matter?
Am I living according to what I believe, or am I a
    hypocrite just waiting to be found out?

Practitioners of psychiatry and psychology have spent years trying to discover the essence of our humanity. In truth, they have come a long way. They must be given credit. In describing the emotional side of men and women, they have made discoveries that have challenged tradition. In astounding ways, they have truly come to understand the emotional makeup of the human brain.

But is emotion all there is?

If I were to ask you today, "Who are you?" how would you respond? Think about it. How would you describe yourself?

I'm guessing you would start by telling me your name. If I were to dig a little deeper, you might tell me about your family. You're a mother of four. An overworked father. An only child. Maybe you would tell me something about your beliefs or your lifestyle. You're a Catholic or a Protestant. An atheist, agnostic, evolutionist, or creationist. An environmentalist or an animal-rights activist. An extrovert or an introvert. Maybe you would take the political route and tell me you're a Republican or a Democrat, conservative or liberal or progressive. Or maybe you would tell me about your ancestry—you're American, Latin, African, or Norwegian. (My grandfather always enjoyed telling people he was Scotch-Presbyterian, though I think he preferred the "scotch" to the Presbyterian.)

If I asked who you are, you could answer any number of ways. But would it fully describe you? Do you really even know who you are? Do you understand what makes you tick? Think about it.

Deep down, I wonder the same things about myself sometimes. Do I fully know myself? No way! My wife sees nuances I never see in myself.

What is a person anyway? Are we intelligent apes? Where did we *really* come from? Where are we going? And how does it affect us in our daily lives?

When it comes to defining who you are, you may believe any number of things. But the bigger question is this: What does God, your Creator, say about you?

Millions of people wander through life seeking to survive, to find joy and experience peace, only to be left tired, discouraged, and disillusioned. And it's no wonder. Without a foundation in *the truth*, life will suck you dry and leave you weak and depleted. That goes for Christians and non-Christians alike.

Did you know that four out of five Americans today consider themselves Christians?[4] An even larger percentage would say they believe in God. But if you were to ask those same people what it means to be a Christian, I can almost guarantee that you would get many different answers.

Like many others, I grew up attending Sunday school and church. I knew most of the songs and stories, and I could give you all the right answers. I actually enjoyed and revered the Holy Bible. But it took me several years to figure out what it really means to be a Christian—the core of a fulfilled and exciting life. (In many ways, I feel as if I'm still learning.) It wasn't a question of whether my church taught the truth. In fact, the leaders of that small congregation in Argentina were some of the strongest biblical scholars I have ever known. It was my own lack of understanding and my own choices that took so long to come into perspective.

I'm convinced that most people—no matter where they stand on the religious spectrum—are confused about faith. They don't fully understand what faith is all about. Even worse, their faith is doing very little for them in their daily lives.

God wants each of us to know where we stand in his eyes. What does it mean to say you believe in God, and what effect does that belief have on your life? And—just as pertinent—if you don't believe in God, what does that mean for you?

◙   ◙   ◙

Our world has no shortage of belief systems. At times, it feels like a buffet or an ice cream shop—with a plethora of flavors to choose from. Or make up a flavor of your own. And to be quite honest, many times we don't even realize we're doing it.

A few years ago, I visited an atheist friend of mine in China. He is a high government official, well respected, knowledgeable, and dignified. When it comes to the intellect, he is brilliant. I have a high regard for him and truly consider him a friend. We wrote a book together discussing religion, and it was fascinating to hear his views. But one thing he said in our conversations together struck me as odd—and it wasn't the first time I had heard it.

"Most of the major religions," he said, "claim that their god is the only god. I cannot discriminate against any one of them, so I am left with only two choices. The first: I believe all their claims are correct. In that case, there will be many gods, and many contradictions. The second choice is that all the claims are unfounded; there's no God at all. No religion would agree with me on that, either."

Quite frankly, I'm baffled by that mind-set. And again, I know he's not the only one who thinks that way. Yes, there are many religions out there. Yes, most of them claim that their god is the only true god. But they are not all the same. And they can't be mixed and matched to create a customizable god.

The same truth applies to Bible-believing Christians. Just believing something because it sounds nice isn't good enough. It has to be true. We can't customize God. We can't censor Jesus, paying attention to teachings we like and letting everything else slide. We can't change our faith into something that makes us feel comfortable. We must dig down to bedrock and anchor our faith there. We must study and pray to understand the true reality of our faith and learn to trust in God on a daily basis. Quite frankly, though, many Christians stop short and miss out on huge aspects of their faith in God.

The truth is out there to be found. I truly believe that. I believe it can be known, and I want to know it. That belief and desire challenge me to dig deep into the Word of God to truly discover the amazing promises and revolutionary life that God offers us.

If Jesus truly is still alive—and that is something I believe wholeheartedly—how does that affect my life today? How does he function—practically and daily—in my life?

Given the hodgepodge of religious beliefs in the world, we need to be aware of what they teach us about ourselves. Whether we realize it or not, these diverse belief systems influence us. Taken all together, they create the climate of faith in which we live, so we had better know what messages they are sending. We had better know if they are grounded in truth.

Just think . . . if I'm a socialist, I'm just a product of my environment. My life is what the world makes of it. If I'm a humanist, I don't believe in God and would have no need for him anyway. Whatever I become, it's because *I* did it. If I'm a materialist, I don't believe I have a soul, and therefore, this entire discussion is pointless. (And you might as well put the book down.) If I'm an evolutionist, I'm just a highly developed ape, a beast left to his beastly ways. If I believe in reincarnation, I'm trapped by karma.

These perspectives all have serious, life-altering implications. They affect the way people view the world, view others, and view themselves. No doubt these views affect culture, entertainment, and our lives, whether we believe them to be true or not. What a person believes makes a powerful difference. Our minds matter, because our thoughts mold our behavior.

In contemporary society, psychologists and psychotherapists have become the new "high priests" in many ways. Along with doctors, counselors, and psychiatrists, therapists can offer treatment for many issues, but they can't answer the ultimate concern—that of human purpose. They can't resolve the nagging issue, the unresolved question floating in the back of our minds—the question of who we really are.

We are more than material creatures. We are more than emotional beings. We are embodied spiritual creatures made in the image of our Creator. To fully understand ourselves, our purpose, our meaning, and our value, we must see the picture as a whole. We must understand our true, full nature. Otherwise, life quickly turns to despair.

◈   ◈   ◈

Some time ago, a friend of one of our sons put a gun to his head and shot himself. He died on the spot. He was only sixteen and the son of a wealthy, notable doctor. It shocked us all. How could this teenager, who seemed to be no different from any other high school student, make such a rash and drastic decision to take his own life?

A few months after the suicide of that boy, our local newspaper reported that a well-known clinical psychologist in town had taken his own life as well. He left this note for his staff: "Tonight I feel tired, alone, and suddenly very old. The full understanding of these feelings will come only when you, too, are tired, alone, and old."

What sadness! Both individuals quite clearly did not see the big picture. They were stuck in the now—focused on the present. The one, a teenager full of possibilities. The other, a highly respected, accomplished professional. And they had no idea how Jesus could have changed their lives. Their view of reality was tainted, and that was enough to push them over the edge. What a waste of life.

The world will wear you down, no question. And if you don't see the whole picture, if you don't understand your full reason for existence—the true reality of Jesus' impact on your life today—you are sure to come to ruin quite quickly.

We're not playing games here. This is your life we're dealing with! This is reality, a matter of life and death—literally. And it has eternal consequences.

If there is something out there I need to know before I die, a reality I am missing in my spiritual life, something that will give me peace, assurance, understanding, and strength, I want to know it! Don't you?

But even more important, if there is assurance, understanding, and truth that will affect my eternal destiny, shouldn't it have an effect on my life right now as well?

Jesus doesn't just save us from our sins and the compounding guilt associated with such a life. He doesn't just give us an assurance of salvation when we die. He offers a lot more than that. In his own words, "I am the gate. Those who come in through me will be saved. . . . My purpose is to give them a rich and satisfying life" (John 10:9-10).

What Jesus offers us is huge! The only question is whether we will take advantage of it—or whether we even realize its truth.

Jesus came to lift you from the ash heap (1 Samuel 2:8, NIV). He has come to rescue you today—right now. You are offered a life worthy of God's high calling. You have more coming to you by God's goodness than you've probably ever realized. God wants to "accomplish infinitely more than we might ask or think" (Ephesians 3:20). So why don't you give Jesus a chance to do it in *your* life?

Sadly, even many committed Christians struggle to know how Jesus can truly transform their lives. Even "strong believers" have doubts, concerns, and unresolved worries. Deep down, when everything is quiet, they truly wonder how it all plays out.

We're far from perfect, and we all know it.

So what is the big picture? What is the truth? How do we gain perspective? More important, where do we look when our world begins to crumble? My desire in these next several chapters is to remind you of some powerful realities, to encourage you with some wonderful promises, and to show you the way of radical, life-changing transformation.

3

BETTER BY FAR

IN DECEMBER 1944—JUST one week before Christmas—my world crumbled as never before. I was ten years old, attending a British boarding school just outside Buenos Aires, the capital city of Argentina. My father, who was a tough businessman, was convinced I needed to learn discipline, structure, and the English language. He was right.

I had just taken final exams during my third year at Quilmes Preparatory School and was getting ready to go home for the holidays. Summer was in full swing (December is summer in Argentina), and I couldn't wait for a few weeks of fun with my friends and family. I also wanted to see my father. He and I had become very close over the past few years, and I loved spending time with him. He had given me a small plot of land in the backyard and was teaching me how to farm. He'd also bought me a horse and was showing me how to ride. I loved my father more than anything.

While classes were in session, I seldom saw or spoke to my family. Even though I was only ten, it was understood that when I was at school, that was my focus. That's why, on that sticky summer morning, my grandmother's phone call caught me by surprise. I immediately knew that something was wrong.

She wasted no time in telling me the news. "Luis, your father is very sick. We really have to pray for him."

My heart fell to the floor.

Grandma gave me no details, but I had a terrible feeling that my father was already dead, or at least dying. The next morning, Grandma came to put me on a train bound for home.

"It's serious," she said as she helped me quickly gather my things. "Your mom wants you to come and see your father immediately."

I wasted no time in beginning the three-hour journey to our home in the small town of Ingeniero Maschwitz—a ride that seemed interminable. I had to take the train into Buenos Aires, catch the underground through town, and grab another train on the other side. For a ten-year-old boy, it was a major task. On most trips home, I took great pleasure in the adventure. It made me feel grown-up and responsible. But on that particular day, I wanted it over before it even started. I wanted to be with my dad.

As I sat alone on the train, I dreamed of taking over the controls and speeding things up in some way. I loved my dad more than ever. We had made plans, and he had promised me so much. To think that something might happen to him was too much for my brain to handle.

I sat in silence, staring ahead yet seeing nothing. There was no way I could ignore the dread, the certainty that I would arrive too late to say good-bye to my father.

When the train finally reached my hometown, I bolted out of my seat and pressed toward the front. When the doors finally opened, I squeezed through as quickly as possible, bounded down the steps, and ran for home.

Any shred of hope I might have harbored in the back of my mind during the long train ride was quickly dispelled when I came within earshot of my house and heard the traditional wailing of mourners. My dad was already gone.

I ran through the gate and up to the door; I was inside before my mother even knew I was home. And there was my father, lying in bed as if asleep.

I ran to him, ignoring my sisters and my other relatives. He had died a few hours earlier, and now his body was yellow and bloated, still secreting fluid, blood drying, lips cracked.

I tried to steel myself amid the crying and sobbing, but I began to shake uncontrollably. I couldn't believe it. I would never talk with my father again. He looked terrible, but I wanted him to be all right. I hugged him and kissed him, but he was gone. No matter what I tried, I would get no response from my father ever again.

My mother, still stunned but not crying, stepped behind me and put her hands on my shoulders. "Lusito," she said softly, pulling me away. "I must talk to you and tell you how it was."

Several days prior, my father had been working out at the docks. He was a businessman—a home developer—and he had just purchased his own barges to shuttle sand and supplies from Paraguay down to Argentina. One of the first shipments of sand had arrived, and as he was in the habit of doing, my father pitched in to make the work of unloading it go quicker.

It was a hot afternoon, and he wasn't prepared for the hard work. He should have known better, but he was too committed. Within a few days, sickness set in. At first, they thought it was nothing more than a cold or flu—nothing to be worried about. My father tried to rest and took a few herbal remedies to fight off the virus. But the cold quickly turned more serious. He couldn't kick the nagging cough, and the fever was uncontrollable.

By the time my father went to see a doctor at the hospital several days later, there was nothing they could do for him. The diagnosis was clear—bronchial pneumonia, the doctor declared—and December 1944 was not a good time to need penicillin. It was all being used overseas, for soldiers who were fighting World War II.

The doctor sent my father home. It was all he knew to do. "At least that way," the doctor reasoned, "he can die in peace surrounded by family." And that's exactly what he did.

My mother and I stood outside—the sun beaming

down—as she recounted my father's last few hours. Looking back, I realize that it was probably more than a ten-year-old boy should hear. But I wanted to know, so she told me. I tried to stifle my sobs while listening to her account, but I wasn't doing a very good job.

For days he had been lying in bed, struggling to keep his fever down and his coughing to a minimum. But he knew the end was near.

Finally, on December 17, as the sun was just peering into the bedroom window, my father's life on earth came to an end. Much of the family was sitting at his bedside, waiting for the inevitable and doing their best to encourage and comfort one another. My four little sisters were there as well, my mother doing her best to protect them from the pain. She herself was struggling, and she was four months pregnant with my youngest sister.

"As we gathered around his bedside," she said, "praying and trying to comfort him, he seemed to fall asleep. He was struggling to breathe, but suddenly he sat up and began to sing." I looked up at my mother, hardly believing what she was telling me.

The song was quite familiar, an old Salvation Army hymn that was one of his favorites:

Bright crowns up there,
bright crowns for you and me.
Then the palm of victory,
the palm of victory.

As he finished the song—exhausted from the galloping fever—he let his head fall back onto his pillow. Then he pointed up to the sky and in a quiet yet determined voice, quoted the apostle Paul from the book of Philippians: "I am going to be with the Lord Jesus, 'which is better by far.'"[5]

With that, he was gone. And I was crushed.

He was thirty-four years old.

⊡ ⊡ ⊡

My father's death turned my world upside down. Not only did it leave the family in pain and agony over his loss, but it also stood as a powerful example and challenge to me personally. It took everything I knew about death and dying and completely turned it on its head. Not only did death become the ultimate reality for me, it became a gauge for life. The brevity of life. The finality of death—this side of eternity, of course.

Everything else can be rationalized, wondered about, and discussed. But death is permanent. Death stares us in the face on a daily basis. As a ten-year-old boy, I sensed that death was staring *me* in the face. It was changing my life. It was real. *It is real!* My father was with us one minute, and gone the next. And that's it. From the perspective of those left behind, when you're gone, you're gone. But where did he go?

My mother's account of that hot summer morning is still so vivid in my mind that I sometimes feel as if I had been there when my father was singing. It still brings tears to my eyes every time I tell the story—even after sixty-plus years. What a man. What a story. His death was such a contrast to the typical Latin American experience, and even as a little boy I noticed it.

In the neighborhood where I grew up, everyone knew when someone was dying. In those days, most people were sent home for their last few days or hours of life. They would lie in bed, with family surrounding, and wail at the top of their lungs. Eerie, I know. But true.

I vividly remember one man's death. He was a close neighbor—just a few doors down. His house was no more than forty yards away from ours. I was a teenager at the time, and the sounds are still seared into my memory. For hours, I heard him screaming, *"I'm dying! I'm dying! I'm going to hell and no one can stop me!"*

I'm telling you, that haunted me for ages. It still gives me chills even today. To hear someone that desperate, that afraid to die—what a reality check! And he wasn't the only one. Most everyone in my town seemed to die like that—fearing the absolute worst. Everyone except my father. The contrast was striking.

I can only imagine the fear those people lived with on a daily basis. Death no doubt consumed a large portion of their thought life as the end neared. But we all wonder about it. We all nervously whistle past the graveyard, imagining where those people are and what it will be like for us when our time comes. And make no mistake, our time will come. I don't want to ignore death, but I don't want to cower in fear either. I want to face it head-on, with conviction and strength—just like my father did.

For many people, death comes too soon, before they're ready. It attacks boys and girls. It lays claim to orphans in Haiti, to islanders in Indonesia, to brothers and sisters in New Orleans. Death and tragedy arrive when we least expect them. Planes drop out of the sky. Earthquakes or tsunamis hit. Diseases strike. Accidents claim lives. Even the strongest and ablest among us is only a heartbeat or a breath away from death.

So what do you make of that reality? What do you do when you know that death is only a matter of time? It will come to you—and to me—at some point.

Here's what I believe is the answer: You resolve to make your life count. You determine to live life as best you know how until you are called home. Like my father, you strive for greatness, in the power of Jesus Christ, every day of your life. You dedicate yourself to live up to your full potential, so that when you arrive in heaven, Jesus will greet you with the precious, priceless words, "Well done, good and faithful servant. . . . Enter into the joy of your lord" (Matthew 25:21, NKJV).

Sadly, many people miss the mark—religious and nonreligious people alike. They ignore the truth, forget the basics, and question what has already been clearly shown to them. They look for acceptance, approval, and meaning in other places. They search for love and power, only to be left empty-handed. They live pointless, mundane lives. And life passes them by.

Let's not be shortsighted. Faith in Jesus Christ is not just a "get out of jail free" card to be used when we stand before the judgment seat. It's not "fire insurance," as so many jokingly call it. We can't make that mistake. There is so much more to our faith today—right now.

I don't have all the answers, but after all these years of life, I've come to realize that the reality of living a truly transformed life is available to *everyone*. I've seen it in the life of my father, in myself, and in tens of thousands of others across seventy-five nations. Regardless of whether your life is cut short or you have the joy of many years on earth, you have the potential for greatness, the ingredients for significance . . . if you handle life as our Creator designed it to be.

Quite frankly, it's not as complicated as we make it out to be. A meaningful, revolutionary life is within our reach. We have the truth. It's just a matter of connecting the dots. It's a matter of believing the Bible—of taking it at face value. And if you have trusted Jesus with your life, you can't forget that "the Spirit of God, who raised Jesus from the dead, lives in you. And just as God raised Christ Jesus from the dead, he will give life to your mortal bodies by this same Spirit living within you" (Romans 8:11).

The solution to death is *life*. And life comes through the powerful transformation available through the work of the Holy Spirit in our hearts. That is the antidote to our often seemingly "dead" lives. That is real living—real transformation. Once we can grasp that reality, we are able to look death in the face and rejoice. After all, we have the same Spirit at work in us that raised Jesus Christ from the dead!

My father's life and death are powerful reminders to me of the truth we are to cling to as Christians. My father lived for Jesus, and he died with Jesus. He focused his entire life—not just a part of it—on the person and power of his Savior, and his life was dramatically changed. It didn't change his circumstances. He still had struggles in life. He still died at age thirty-four. But it shifted his perspective. It realigned his priorities. And it was a transformation that can happen in your life and mine as well.

As much as I want to believe that my father was a super-human spiritual giant, I know he wasn't. He was just like you and me—striving to live a meaningful life on a daily basis. And in the power of Christ, he succeeded. He let the Word of God seep into every aspect of his life. He trusted it at face value and lived according to its principles. And he believed wholeheartedly in the promises of his Savior. It's an example—and challenge—for all of us. "For God has not given us a spirit of fear and timidity, but of power, love, and self-discipline" (2 Timothy 1:7). And that, my friend, is a powerful gift, no matter what circumstances you are facing.

You too can have the same victory my father experienced. You can—and will—see changes in your life when you realize that your life is not your own.

If you have committed yourself to Jesus Christ, your life is in him and him alone.

4

HAPPY AND BLESSED

AFTER MY FATHER'S death, my family struggled financially. It took only a few years for us to lose just about everything. My mother tried to run the family business—bless her heart, she did the best she could—but she was no businesswoman. People took advantage of her. They lied to her face and robbed her blind.

The business that had grown to include a farm, land, trucks, and barges soon dwindled to nothing. I had to quit my studies and take a job in a British corporation in Buenos Aires just to make ends meet. We had bills stacking up—debt beyond our imagination. Thankfully, my bilingual skills were a hot commodity in Argentina at the time, which gave me an open door into a financial career that paid well. I soon became the sole provider for our family of seven and we slowly began digging ourselves out from beneath the massive debt.

Although I had a well-paying job, I couldn't support all seven of us at the level to which we had become accustomed when my father was alive. We learned what it was like to go without. Many nights, our meal consisted of nothing more than a loaf of French bread—one loaf split seven ways. On a good night, we could add a tomato or a small cut of meat, divided into seven little pieces. (You should have seen us— seven skinny Argentines, struggling to survive.)

Life wasn't easy, especially for my mother. Many nights, I found her alone in her room, sobbing into her hands. At first, I didn't get it. After all, she still had all of us kids. Later on, I realized it was probably *because* of us kids that she was sobbing. (Six little monsters—I don't know how she did it.)

All we had left to hold on to was each other and the faith in God we had learned from our mother and father. Quite surprisingly, it was more than enough. In spite of everything, we were joyful. We were happy. Truly, we were! We had come to understand—at least in part—the powerful reality of Jesus' promise from Hebrews 13:5—"I will never fail you. I will never abandon you." It hadn't always been that clear for my father, however. He had known the truth that comforted him in his dying days only during the last ten years of his life.

My father had come to Argentina from Spain with his family when he was twelve years old. They had arrived with next to nothing—just a few clothes and some other belongings. My father was the second oldest of six kids—four boys and two girls.

Four years after they arrived in Argentina, my grandfather died. And just as his own son would do less than twenty-five years later, my father, at age sixteen, became the sole provider for his family.

He met my mother when he was twenty and she was eighteen. He had already established himself as a rather successful home developer in their small town. The two married in 1934, and I was born less than a year later—the first of six children. It was me and five younger sisters. (A half brother joined the family years later.)

My father was a typical guy—a man's man. He wasn't interested in religion and didn't go to church. He didn't think much about life after death. In fact, he didn't think much about life outside of work. He was a businessman—and a good one. He had a staff of several dozen, along with cars and drivers, livestock and land, caretakers, a fleet of trucks, and even river barges. Only one other businessman in our town was more successful. My father was an entrepreneur through and through, and would be until his death. But in 1934, he met Mr. Edward Charles Rogers, whose influence truly changed his life forever.

Mr. Rogers was a businessman as well. He had come from England a few years prior—an executive for one of the big international oil companies. We called him The Missionary because he came to Argentina with the express purpose to win people to Jesus Christ. He had married the daughter of an English missionary in the area, and together they went from door to door sharing the gospel at night after work. That's how we first met Mr. Rogers.

My mother had been the one to answer the door when Mr. Rogers first arrived on our doorstep in 1934—just months after my parents had married. She was intrigued by what he said, began reading the Bible he gave her, and quickly committed her life to Jesus Christ. It was as simple as that. He offered her nothing besides the gospel. No get-rich-quick scheme. No free handouts. No promises of an easier life. Just the freedom found in the Bible. When my mother came across verses such as Matthew 5:8 ("Blessed are the pure in heart, for they will see God," NIV) and John 1:29 ("Look, the Lamb of God, who takes away the sin of the world," NIV), she couldn't help but respond. It was more than enough for her, and her conscience was truly released.

My grandmother also became a Christian soon after, but my father was not won over so easily. He was intrigued by Mr. Rogers, but he made it clear that he wanted nothing to do with religion or the gospel. It wasn't that he didn't believe. More likely, he just didn't care. He had better things to do. He had a business to grow. He had a life to live. He had a family to provide for. He was a good man, no question. He had never done anything truly illegal or bad. And he desired to live a good life. But he didn't have time for religion or the rules that came with it. It just didn't seem to make sense.

If you had asked him at the time, my father probably

would have said he was religious. It just didn't affect his everyday life. It wasn't something he thought about or cared for on a daily basis. (He played soccer on Sunday mornings, and that was more important.)

Then one day, months after my mother's conversion, my father surprised the entire community. After seeing my mother's life completely transformed, he wanted to hear more about this person Jesus. Sure, he knew who Jesus was. But it almost seemed as if my mother knew a completely different Jesus—one who was relevant and active and interested in her life. A Jesus who was actually alive and active.

When he dropped my mother off at church one Sunday evening, my father decided to follow her inside. Without a word, he sat down next to her. (She later found out that he had been standing outside the chapel listening to the messages for weeks.) As always, Mr. Rogers and the leaders of the small church shared the gospel clearly and directly. It wasn't sugarcoated. It wasn't even that eloquent. But it was effective. That night, the sermon was drawn from 1 Corinthians 15:1-3:

> Let me now remind you, dear brothers and sisters,
> of the Good News I preached to you before. You
> welcomed it then, and you still stand firm in it. It
> is this Good News that saves you if you continue to
> believe the message I told you—unless, of course,
> you believed something that was never true in the
> first place.

> I passed on to you what was most important and
> what had also been passed on to me. Christ died for
> our sins, just as the Scriptures said.

Several minutes into the message, as Mr. Rogers was further
explaining the text, my father stood up and interrupted the
lesson. He was a gentleman about it, but he was firm. "Right
now," he said, "I receive Jesus Christ as my only and sufficient Savior."

And then he sat down.

Mr. Rogers was so startled that he stopped preaching for
a few moments. My mother was nearly underneath her seat,
cringing from embarrassment yet jumping for joy inside.

Talk about a radical transformation! From that point on,
my father never looked back. He was convinced. He was a
man of purpose, intention, and conviction. He had just met
the real Jesus—the one who is active and powerful and interested in changing our lives—and he had decided to surrender
his life to the Lord's leading.

Within a matter of days, my father was studying the Bible
with Mr. Rogers. He was digging deep into the text, starting
with the Gospel of John and the book of Proverbs. He was
learning what it meant to follow Jesus, and he was using all
his resources to share this amazing truth with others.

For the next nine years, my father was fully committed to
a life of following Jesus Christ, and he relied on the strength
of the Holy Spirit to lead him and guide him. His life was no
longer his own; he had been bought at a price, and he knew

that meant he needed to honor God with his body and his life (1 Corinthians 6:20). He used every spare moment to study the Bible. He used his resources to help people in need and to build other church buildings, and he used his business to bless others as well. In fact, every summer, he and Mr. Rogers—with their families in tow—visited a nearby town or village, sharing the message of Jesus, leading people to receive Christ, building a church, and blessing the community any way they knew how.

In those nine years, my father and Mr. Rogers planted nine churches. And those churches are still there today—both the congregations and the buildings my father built. Sure, they had opposition. I was there as a boy. I saw how difficult it was. I heard the names some of the villagers called my father. I was a witness to the insults and the rock throwing. (I remember so badly wanting to throw rocks back at the hecklers, but of course my father wouldn't let me.)

No matter the insults, arguments, or stories, no one could question—or would question—my father's transformation, conviction, and tender heart. Those same people who threw rocks at him (literally, they threw rocks!) were the ones he cared the most about. It was for them that he visited those towns and villages. He harbored no ill will toward them. He prayed for them continually. He wanted what was best for them. And today—for those who still remember my father—the testimony of his life is what stands out.

But then he died. Without warning, he was gone. His earthly life was over.

Speaking with friends, family, and acquaintances over the years, I have come to realize what a drastic change it was for my father to begin believing in Jesus Christ. He became a Christian when I was still just a baby, so I didn't know any different. But from what I can tell and what others tell me, the transformation was astounding.

Almost as if overnight, I'm told, my father's priorities changed. His focus shifted and his determination grew stronger. (His friends joked that, when he was converted, his pocketbook was converted as well.) He became even more successful in his business, and he used his resources to further God's causes. He began reaching out, serving the needy, and sharing with others. And more than nine towns were blessed by his life. In fact, they are still blessed today as a result. Although his life was cut short, his legacy lives on.

Just a few years ago, I visited one of those nine towns. It was off the beaten path when my father was there seventy years ago, and it's still off the beaten path today. I had been in town for less than five minutes when an old man stopped me on the street.

"You're Mr. Palau, aren't you?" he said. "I remember your father. He was a good man. Do you want to see the church he built?"

At that, he led me past a large church to a small field behind. He pointed to a small ten-foot by twenty-foot slab of concrete in the middle of the field. "That's the foundation of the church your father built seventy years ago," he explained. "That is where we met for years."

Then he turned and pointed to the larger church building we had just walked past. "But our congregation got too big. We outgrew the building and it was getting old. Now we meet here."

I couldn't keep myself from crying. This town—out of the way and forgotten by much of the world—had been blessed by my father. He cared about the people, and they knew it. Now, seven decades later, the church he had helped plant was not only continuing, but it was growing. It will probably outlive us all. One of the leaders—a friend from my youth—told me that out of my dad's ministry and the churches he helped to plant, forty-two missionaries, Bible teachers, and evangelists (including me) went out as full-time Christian workers.

Looking back on my father's life, his death, and his overwhelming passion for others, I find that one thing is clear: He had something that most in my town did not. He had a revolutionary faith. He had a faith that permeated his entire being. He had a faith that was real. Why? Because he was willing to step out and live according to his convictions. He was willing to fear God more than man. He was willing to adjust his priorities, to make God's goals his goals, and to see the world the way the Lord sees it—lost and in desperate need of hope.

My dad was willing to put God first in everything. He was willing to use his resources for God's glory, to set aside his own life, and to do what the Lord had called him to do.

If there is one thing I've learned in my years of ministry, it's that my father's story is not unique. It's rare, but it is definitely repeatable. And it all starts with ordinary people—businessmen, young mothers, students, couples, and singles—people willing to listen to the truth of Jesus Christ and actually let it redirect their lives. It starts with people willing to discover the real Jesus and the revolutionary life he offers us. People willing to trade in their ashes for beauty; to pick up their own crosses and follow after their Savior.

Like my father, we all need to count the cost. We need to be willing to set aside our own agendas and realize that our lives are no longer our own. (I know that's a tough thing to hear.) We need to be willing to trust God, to step out in faith, to bear our crosses, to take on Christ's burdens, and to follow after him. It may sound difficult, and at times it is. But as my father found for himself, and I have come to learn as well, there is no life worth living outside of the cause of Christ. His priorities must be our own. His life must be ours. Otherwise, we cannot be his disciples.

> But don't begin until you count the cost. For who would begin construction of a building without first calculating the cost to see if there is enough money to finish it? Otherwise, you might complete only the foundation before running out of money, and then everyone would laugh at you. They would say, "There's the person who started that building and couldn't afford to finish it!" (Luke 14:28-30)

How many have built a foundation on God, only to leave it unattended and unfinished? How many have started a race of faith, only to find themselves standing on the sidelines? Let it not be so for you! You say you trust in God, but do your actions tell a different story? We can't afford not to finish what we have started.

I can't wait to see my father again in heaven. I know he'll be there. I know he'll be waiting with open arms. And I can't wait to thank him for the example he left—for the cross he bore. He paved the way for me. He gave me a glimmer of hope. He challenged me—and is challenging you as well—to fight the good fight, to stand with Jesus, and to put everything on the line for God's glory, not your own.

After all, the world becomes a scary place if we're left to our own devices. But not if we live daily with eternity's values in view.

5

MONSTERS OF DEPRAVITY

"If I set down every action in my life and every thought that has crossed my mind, the world would consider me a monster of depravity."[6] The first time I read that quote, in a magazine article about writer Somerset Maugham, the phrase jumped off the page at me. I had never thought of my life that way, but it had the ring of truth. The more I thought about it, the more appalled I became. It was quite true—at least for me.

You'll often hear it said that someone is a "good person." But what does that really mean? Could it be that "good" people are simply better at covering up their inner depravity? The longer I live and the more I experience, the more convinced

I am that depravity—utter moral corruption—resides in the heart of every human being. Sadly, many people's lives are controlled and destroyed by this inner corruption.

When we're all left sober with our thoughts (as my son Andrew likes to say), it's a *sobering* reality. We aren't as perfect as we try to portray to the world. We don't have it all together. We're messed up—each and every one of us. We have our skeletons in the closet. We have our buried secrets that we try to keep covered. And we spend a lot of time praying that no one finds out. Apart from God, our souls and our spirits are in shambles, and we have no hope and no clue what to do.

❖　　❖　　❖

Several years ago, Patricia and I were invited to vacation at the home of some friends in Southern California. They had a beautiful house with plenty of space, a super swimming pool, and gorgeous views of the Pacific Ocean and the surrounding area. Though they would be home—along with their grown daughter—they assured us that while we were there they would leave us alone and let us rest. It had been a long year for us, and we were looking forward to a little quiet respite with our four sons.

We agreed—never wanting to turn down a free vacation—and joined them at their home. It took only a few hours, though, for the desperate plea to come out.

"Look," they said, "we know you two are on vacation. We

know you want to be left alone, and we know that's what we promised. But we desperately need your help."

That's how our vacation began.

"Please," they urged, "our daughter Sarah is in such pain. The last few years have been a nightmare for her. Her marriage has fallen apart. Guilt is eating her up inside. She has fallen away from God. She thinks she has lost her salvation. She's seeing a psychiatrist twice a month, and she's at her wits' end. Please, could you meet with her . . . talk with her . . . do whatever you can to help her?"

We could tell they were desperate. We could see it in their eyes.

Patricia and I agreed that we would meet with our friends and their daughter for breakfast on Saturday morning.

Saturday couldn't come soon enough for our friends. They wanted so desperately to help their daughter. As we finished breakfast, we asked the parents to give us some time alone with Sarah.

This beautiful young woman, twenty-five years old, was so sweet and sensitive. You could tell she had a brilliant mind. Until recently, she had been making a good living as a surgical nurse. But now she was so lost and broken that she was unable to work.

As we talked, Sarah slowly began to open up to my wife and me, and inevitably the conversation turned to her pain. As we dug deeper into her life, she shared her heart-wrenching story with us.

Just out of university, Sarah had met Caleb, a confident,

debonair, young navy officer. They hit it off, began dating, and quickly got married. Both were churchgoers from fine homes, and both followed Jesus. They seemed to be the perfect match.

Soon after the wedding, Caleb was sent to a naval base out of state. He and Sarah moved there together and really were doing quite well. But six months into their marriage, they received a phone call from one of Caleb's buddies from school. John had some vacation time and was itching to find some sun. He asked if he could stay at their place for a few weeks.

Naturally, the young couple agreed, and they were happy to do so. This was one of Caleb's close friends, and they wanted to show him the area around their new home. Caleb decided he would take two weeks off, giving him time to show John the sights and play some golf, and of course make it less awkward for Sarah, who wasn't working at the time.

The first week that John was in town, Caleb still had to work, so it fell to Sarah to show John around. As you can imagine, it was awkward at first. She didn't know him from Adam. But as they drove around town together, they quickly warmed up to one another. By day two, they were more than comfortable, and Sarah had no problem showing John the sights.

She did her best to make him feel at home, taking him shopping and to the beautiful beaches—what any normal person would do. But as they became more accustomed to each other, Sarah noticed John's attitude and attention shifting. By day four, John was more interested in her than in the sights. He began to subtly flirt with Sarah.

At first, she laughed it off as immature niceties. After all, she didn't want to think ill of Caleb's friend. But it didn't take long for John to take it a step further. The next day, he began making overt comments, telling her how beautiful she was and commenting on how lonely she must be. Sarah did her best to resist the flattery, but by day six, she was utterly mesmerized. That's when she and John ended up on the couch. Before she knew it, she had done the unthinkable. While her husband was at work, she committed adultery with one of his closest friends.

Of course, Sarah immediately knew that what she had done was wrong . . . very wrong. She knew she had to do something. As soon as Caleb came home that night, she flipped out. Without explanation, she said to Caleb, "Get John out of here. Send him back home. I can't stand him and I want him out of our house."

Of course, her husband was confused. He prodded a little, but she wasn't about to tell him the truth. When she didn't respond with anything more than vague "concerns," Caleb shrugged it off and disregarded her request. After all, he hadn't even had time to see his friend or do the things they had planned.

For two days, Sarah tried to persuade Caleb to send John back home. But it was no use. Without knowing the full story, Caleb wasn't going to budge. So Sarah finally spilled her story and confessed her guilt. She told Caleb everything. She knew it would hurt him, but she couldn't think of a better way.

"Forgive me," she said as they were alone in their bedroom.

"I slept with your friend. I know it was wrong. I know I'm horrible. I love *you*! I gave in and I shouldn't have." She was sobbing by now, desperate for her husband's forgiveness. But it was too late. The damage had been done.

Caleb was livid. He could barely look at her. Instead of sending his buddy home as she had requested, Caleb sent Sarah packing, back to her parents in Southern California. She was rejected, broken, and guilt-ridden. And that's how Patricia and I found her—divorced, ashamed, in pain, and on the verge of a total emotional breakdown.

In the midst of her sobs, we did our best to comfort her. Sarah was obviously repentant of her sinful behavior. I tried to share the truth with her and encourage her. "Yes, it was horrible what you did. Yes, you have paid dearly for it. Yes, you now are divorced, you're lonely, and you're in pain. But you don't have to go on feeling that way."

For nearly three hours, we shared key verses from the Bible with her. We reminded her that if she believed in God, if she trusted in Jesus Christ, if she asked for forgiveness, she could be washed clean.

We reminded her of Hebrews 10:17: "I will never again remember [your] sins and lawless deeds." But she couldn't shake the guilt. Like a broken record, she kept repeating, "But I did it. I knew it was wrong. I broke God's moral law. I *knew* it was wrong and I did it anyway!"

We repeatedly responded with God's promise: "I will never again remember your sins and lawless deeds."

I could feel the weight of the guilt that had taken over

her life. It's the same guilt—mixed with shame—that plagues many people today.

◙   ◙   ◙

Sure, there are still people who insist that we're all good at heart. It's pretty common for people to believe that innocence and goodness well up inside each and every one of us, even from a very young age. In fact, someone recently told me, "If you want to see the essence of innocence—the purity of life—go and watch children on the playground."

I'm sorry, but I don't see innocence on a playground. Sure, they are cute. But I see greed. I see selfishness. I see temper tantrums and meltdowns. I see the true essence of our humanity, and it's not as pretty as many people wish it would be.

Sadly, our world today is not what the Lord intended. Our lives are not as God designed them to be. We don't act as if we are made in the image of God. We are all "monsters of depravity."

If you were to write down every thought that ever crossed your mind, every deed you've ever done, you'd have the makings of a best seller for sure! Just think—every crass remark about your coworkers, every snide comment about that driver in the car in front of you, every glance in the wrong direction, every hateful thought toward your spouse or your child, every lustful idea about that neighbor or friend. What about that little white lie, or that corner you cut; that illegal deal no one found out about, or that Web site you visit every once in a while when no one is looking?

If you wrote down everything for the world to see, your spouse would probably leave you before the day was out. Your friends would probably stop talking to you. Your mother-in-law would disown you for sure.

I don't doubt that most people have *good intentions*. But we're far from perfect. In fact, the Bible describes our situation this way: "The heart is deceitful above all things, and desperately wicked; who can know it?" (Jeremiah 17:9, NKJV). And "all have sinned and fall short of the glory of God" (Romans 3:23, NIV).

Even secular philosophers and Nobel Prize winners acknowledge the truth about the human condition. Many even paint the picture a darker shade of gray. Jean-Paul Sartre, the great French philosopher (also known as the philosopher of despair) believed there was "no exit" from the human dilemma: "Man . . . is alone, abandoned on earth . . . , with no other destiny than the one he forges for himself on this earth."[7] And I once heard Nobel Prize–winner Elie Wiesel put it this way: "I have looked into the heart of man and I stared in the face of evil."

The Bible doesn't teach that man was created sinful or imperfect. In fact, God was pleased when he first created man. But it didn't take long for us to sin. And we've been causing trouble ever since. Each one of us—like Sarah—has chosen sin. Be it little or big, we have chosen evil more than once in our lives.

Never has this reality been more apparent to me than in the past few years. As the world economy has been shaken around us, we've watched firsthand as brilliant, Ivy League–trained, first-rate businessmen have been ushered off to jail. I don't have to point to crime in low-income areas to prove my point anymore. Just look at some of the indicted men of Wall Street. These are educated, learned people! They should know better. We should all know better.

Paul, the writer of Romans, puts it this way, "We know that the law is spiritual; but I am unspiritual, sold as a slave to sin. I do not understand what I do. For what I want to do I do not do, but what I hate I do" (Romans 7:14-15, NIV).

We are all sinners. We are all greedy. Education doesn't take it out of us. A good upbringing doesn't cure us. Sitting in church doesn't heal us. Our sinful nature is rooted much deeper within.

As we come to terms with this reality, we must recognize what we're really up against and where it leaves us: guilty and guilt-ridden, just like Sarah.

◆   ◆   ◆

As an evangelist, I travel a lot. I seem to always be on an airplane. Over the years, I have found myself sitting next to a number of psychologists, psychiatrists, counselors, doctors, and therapists. I love it. Whenever I find myself next to someone in the field of psychology, I have to ask, "What is the number one reason that people come to see you?" (If nothing else, I'm curious why people spend money to tell a stranger their problems.)

It never fails. In forty-plus years of asking mental health care professionals that question, the answer is always the same. The reason for 80 percent of the cases they see? *Unresolved guilt!*

That's fascinating to me—fascinating and sad. The number one reason why people visit counselors, psychologists, psychiatrists, and therapists—why they spend exorbitant amounts of money to sit and talk with a stranger—is because of unresolved guilt. Why is that? Because we know we have a problem, and we don't know how to fix it. You hear it in the apostle Paul's words. Just look at them again:

"What I want to do I do not do, but what I hate I do."

In essence, we all have a spiritual cancer eating away at us. Deep down, we have a problem—a dead spirit and an aching conscience. If left unattended, it leads to despair. It's why some people drink. It's why many take drugs, abuse relationships, overeat, or hide emotionally from other people. They're trying to cover the pain.

What about you? Where has your sin—your unresolved guilt—left you?

For Sarah, it had left her broken and in pain. And it wasn't just her own sin that was ruining her life. She was bearing the weight of many sins on her shoulders—her husband's unwillingness to forgive, John's unchecked lustful desires, and her own surrender. Sarah didn't have the luxury of a closet in which to hide her skeletons. Her secrets were out there for the world to see. And the pain was unbearable.

◈　　◈　　◈

Unfortunately, millions of people around the world share Sarah's uncertainty, shame, and guilt. Why? Because they are trusting their own efforts to get them into paradise. This kind of thinking permeates all religions, including traditional (but unbiblical) Christianity.

From the moment Adam disobeyed God in the Garden of Eden, we have been seeking a way to cover our sins and cleanse our consciences. We desire to do well, yet we fail miserably. We seek healing, yet find guilt. We struggle wholeheartedly to learn what it will take—what we must do—to find true healing from the pain. We petition God. And God has always replied, "There's nothing you can do. You must trust me to do it for you."

Sarah could have sat in counseling for years, and it probably would have helped on a certain level. But what she really needed that Saturday morning—what her heart really was crying for—was for Jesus to show up. She needed the Great Physician, the only one willing *and able* to completely rid her conscience of shame and guilt, the only one able to offer true healing. And the fact is, he had been there all along. I knew exactly where to turn.

I flipped the pages of my Bible to 1 Peter 2:24. Looking straight into Sarah's watery eyes, I told her with as much confidence, force, and love as I could muster, "Sarah, you *must* listen to this."

At that, I began reading slowly and methodically: "Sarah, this is what the Bible says: 'He *himself*'. . . Jesus . . . 'bore our sins in *his* body on the tree, so that *we* might die to sins and *live for righteousness*; by his wounds *you have been healed.*'"[8]

I let the words sink in. Patricia and I prayed they would take hold. They were exactly what Sarah needed to hear. God himself had borne her sins. He had taken the punishment. The shame, the pain, the filth, had been nailed to the cross. Sarah's sins—should she choose to truly put her faith in Jesus—had already been wiped away. His sacrifice was more than sufficient. And by his wounds she had been healed.

As the words from 1 Peter permeated her thoughts, Sarah's demeanor began to soften. I knew she was getting it.

"Sarah, Jesus Christ died for you. He sacrificed his life to take away your sin. He gave his life to make you clean. It's available to you. It's available to you every day! He's waiting for you. And all you have to do is respond to him and ask for his forgiveness, and watch the guilt fall away. He will never again remember your sins and lawless deeds."

I could see it in her tear-streaked eyes. She finally got it. With gentle prompting, Patricia and I led Sarah in a prayer and she opened her heart to Jesus. For the first time since we had met her, I saw hope return.

A month or two after our time with Sarah, as I reflected back on that day, I remembered a beautiful vase her parents had had on display, and I thought of an analogy that might have helped Sarah to see the truth.

The vase, as I recall, truly was exquisite—delicate and wonderfully crafted. The etchings were first rate, the colors vibrant. The potter had clearly invested time in this piece, and the craftsmanship was obvious.

In my mind's eye, I imagined that precious vase covered in mud, as if it had been tossed on a trash heap. It was still the same beautiful vase—intricate, treasured, one-of-a-kind—but its beauty was now obscured by the muck and the grime.

In a sense, we are all like that vase when we fall into sin. The Bible says that we are fearfully and wonderfully made (Psalm 139:14, NIV), but we've all been tarnished and trashed by the dirt and desecration of sin. Apart from God, we have covered ourselves in mud; we have gotten caught up in ugliness and pain. Our true beauty and purpose have been covered by years of destructive, selfish behavior. And we can't seem to see ourselves beyond the dirt.

But the Lord is powerful. He is ready and waiting to wash us clean—to restore us to our original, intended beauty. He has already done the healing work on the cross. He is just waiting to welcome us into his family and make us new.

What does God have to offer someone like Sarah? What does Jesus have to offer you? It's simple, yet profound. He offers freedom from guilt—total forgiveness when we truly repent and confess our inner sinfulness to him.

This is where Jesus Christ shines so beautifully. Let's face it, the main reason why the human race is in trouble—why we have gone to war so many times, why there are so many heartbreaks and family breakups—is because of unresolved guilt. Professional counselors can no doubt help to pinpoint where the problem began; they can help to calm you down with some sort of pill or procedure. But only Jesus can remove the guilt for good. It's what he came to do on the cross, where he was crucified to pay for our guilt.

The promise is clear. We've all heard it. Jesus "offered himself to God as a perfect sacrifice for our sins" in order to "purify our consciences from sinful deeds so that we can worship the living God" (Hebrews 9:14). But that's not all. The writer also reminds us that God "will never again remember [our] sins and lawless deeds" (Hebrews 10:17). That is a flat-out promise from God for everyone who trusts in Jesus Christ and his death on the cross. It's just as true for you as it was, and is, for Sarah.

There is no reason to continue living with guilt. It's destructive. It's unnecessary. Jesus not only died for all of our evil deeds, but he also cast them into the deepest pit. "He has removed our sins as far from us as the east is from the west" (Psalm 103:12). As Corrie ten Boom used to say, "When we confess our sins, God casts them into the deepest ocean, gone forever. . . . I believe God then places a sign out there that says, NO FISHING ALLOWED."[9]

It has been more than fifteen years since my wife and I had that conversation with Sarah. Today, she has been completely transformed. She met a young man in her church—a godly man who had seen how God had worked in her life—and they married. They have a beautiful marriage and a wonderful little boy. She sings in her church choir. It's tremendous! God's therapy is divine therapy. It is "God's peace, which exceeds anything we can understand" (Philippians 4:7). *And it is real!*

Whether your story is similar to Sarah's or not, it may be no less painful. But let me assure you, if you're struggling with a powerful sense of guilt, there is hope. If you're wondering where your life is headed, there is direction to be found. You have the answer. It lies in Jesus Christ. All you have to do is accept his forgiveness on a moment-by-moment basis, and watch where he leads.

6

WHERE YOUR AUTHORITY TRULY LIES

SOME SAY THAT true life comes only once you begin to believe in yourself. Not true. In fact, G. K. Chesterton said it best when he wrote, "I know of men who believe in themselves more colossally than Napoleon or Caesar. . . . I can guide you to the thrones of the Super-men. The men who really believe in themselves are all in lunatic asylums."[10]

It's true. Many unfortunate, confused, and mentally unstable people have a rather high view of themselves. It says nothing about how successful, happy, or fulfilled they are in life. On the contrary, real life comes when you realize that, on your own, you have nothing to offer. True fulfillment comes when you finally understand the way the world really works and submit to the rightful authority—the one who truly knows you. He is your Creator—God Almighty.

If we are going to get serious about this whole "authority" discussion, we need to have a base from which to work. We need a foundation. In this day and age, that can be difficult. For me, I stand firmly on the Bible. I trust in its final authority. But I know that's not the case for everyone. The Bible may actually be a hang-up for you. If so, you're not alone.

Several years ago, I had the opportunity to meet with a dozen ministers in a Western European city where I was involved in a campaign. To say I was shocked by our discussion may be a bit too strong, but I was certainly surprised. At least half of these ministers did not accept the Bible as the authoritative and sufficient Word of God.

Several said they believed that some Scripture passages were erroneous. Others admitted that when they are uncomfortable with portions of the Bible, they rationalize them away as "unscientific."

Is it any wonder that, in certain parts of the world, churches are struggling? Who wants to listen to a minister who doesn't believe the Bible is the Word of God? Where is his or her authority?

The same goes for individual Christians. When the one document we hold so dear is treated like a choose-your-own-adventure story, why do we think the world calls us hypocrites? When we skip some parts of the Bible and cast others out completely, how do we expect anyone to accept the parts we've decided to keep? It doesn't make sense.

Maybe you're in the same boat as these ministers. With so many critics out there, it's hard not to listen to some of the arguments against the authority of the Bible. But quite honestly, they just don't hold weight.

I'm always surprised to hear of the number of Christians who seldom read God's Word. Sure, they take the Bible with them to church on occasion. They carry it under the arm or display it on the coffee table at home. But they don't know where to look to find encouragement or guidance within its pages. They don't really believe that it's a true guidebook for living. After all, if they did, wouldn't they be poring over its pages on a daily basis?

I'm convinced that each one of us needs to give the Word of God—the Bible—a real hearing. Not only is it the number one best-selling book of all time, it has influenced cultures, shaped leaders, defined societies, and dramatically changed millions of people's lives around the world. And the more you dig into it, the more you will realize its power.

The Bible is one of the most beautifully written, historically accurate, and emotionally appealing literary works known to humankind. Many of my atheist friends will attest to that as well. But they sell it short, and I believe they are truly missing out on its real beauty.

The fact is, the Bible offers insight into our existence, perspective into our lives, and moral values that—when followed—revolutionize our world. Christianity alone has proven its relevance and power in all cultures and levels of society. And why? Because it all points back to one person—Jesus Christ.

But maybe you're still not convinced.

Personally, I have no question in my mind that the Bible is true, accurate, and inspired by God. I have no question that the claims of Christianity have the power to transform lives. When you take the Word of God at face value and begin living in accordance with its instruction, you will be transformed!

My friend Dave Hall is a perfect example. For years he "believed" in God. He read the Bible on occasion. Though he would have called himself a Christian, he didn't act on that belief on a daily basis. He didn't need it for daily living . . . or so he thought. And frankly, he had strong reservations about its relevance to his life.

Dave was a self-made man—successful, strong, respected, and winsome. If he wanted to get something done, he did it himself. He competed with the world. He always won. And he enjoyed it. So why would he need God?

It wasn't until he and his wife, Katherine, had children— two beautiful girls—that he began to really think about God. As the girls got older, Dave decided they "needed religion." Even though it wasn't for him, it would be good for them. He and Katherine began taking them to church. And as Dave sat in the pew each Sunday, listening to the Word of God being proclaimed, he began to feel convicted. He slowly dug deeper into Scripture and started asking fundamental questions. He began to search. And what he found was astonishing.

As Dave read the Bible for himself, he was blown away by its accuracy. As he read about the human condition, he knew he was reading about himself, his brokenness, and his flaws. But he was also faced with powerful promises of change. And even more, he was left with a challenge: "What if this is all true?"

For more than two years, Dave sat in church listening to the same Bible-centered messages—consistently calling him to repentance and holy living. He couldn't deny its relevance. But he fought it. If he gave in, it would cause him to change his life, his priorities, and his values. It was too much to ask. So he put on a smile, stayed in church, tossed a few dollars in the offering plate, and lived in quiet rebellion against God. It ate him up inside.

Over those two years, God was working on Dave. Dave's competitive side was becoming overwhelming. He was realizing—deep down—that he truly wasn't content. As he evaluated his life, he began to realize his shortcomings. At the top of the list? His focus on power, wealth, respect, and envy. He knew the returns were empty. And he couldn't shake the powerful words of God he was hearing on a weekly basis. He was feeling pursued.

Finally, Dave showed up at church one week and found television cameras placed throughout the auditorium. He got excited, thinking that a prominent business leader might be the featured speaker of the morning. He was looking forward to another self-made man sharing insights on how to become more successful and how he might reconcile what he was reading. Instead, it was some Argentine evangelist (me), who was preparing to challenge him with the Good News of Jesus Christ. Dave was less than thrilled when I stepped up to the podium.

When Dave recounts the story, he tells it with humor. But there was no joking for him that Sunday morning. The message I shared was direct. And it was exactly what Dave needed to hear. No more games. No more fighting. Just honest living, surrendered to Jesus Christ. Dave was ready to make a change. That was the beginning of a new day for him, committing his entire life to Jesus Christ. Since then, Dave has been radically different.

As Dave looked at his life with new eyes, he began to realize just how confused and disoriented he had become. His priorities were in complete contrast to the teaching of the Bible. His attitude and actions toward others were downright sinful. It was time for a change. Through the working of the Holy Spirit, the Lord began to show Dave his need for compassion for those less fortunate. He learned to look at others not as competitors, but as neighbors—individuals in need of God's love and forgiveness just like he was. He realized there were other ways to win than just beating the competition. And he came to the powerful understanding that his money and his possessions were merely gifts from God. But maybe most important of all, the Lord showed Dave that pursuing the will of God was far more important and fulfilling than feeding his own ego. And that alone would prove revolutionary.

Today, Dave is one of the most compassionate, sincere, and loving men I have ever met. Is he still competitive? Sure. (On the golf course, mostly.) But his passion for people and love for the Word of God are unquestionable. His family is first-rate. His wife is a gem. His legacy is far-reaching. And his testimony for the Lord is powerful. Scores of young success-driven men look to Dave for counsel, prayer, and guidance. And he is gifted.

Today, Dave is chairman of the board of directors for our evangelistic ministry. He has helped reach millions of people with the same life-changing message that transformed him so many years ago. He is active in his church and leads three Bible studies per week. He and his wife are stellar witnesses for Jesus, and their two daughters (now grown and married) lead just as powerful lives. He's still wonderfully successful in business. He still takes his work (and his golf) very seriously. But what defines him—what gives him worth—is his Lord and Savior, Jesus Christ. What leads him is the Bible.

Before, Dave's priorities were happiness and success, followed by his wife and his children. Today, his priorities are God, wife, and children (and grandchildren), then followed by business success. And the funny thing . . . with business and financial success in their rightful place, he has substantially more than before.

For years, Dave believed the Bible to be true. For years he had head knowledge about God, but he didn't really *know* him. He didn't really act on his decision to follow God. After all, it is one thing to say you will follow someone. It's another to actually do it.

❖   ❖   ❖

I truly believe that your view and understanding of Scripture has a direct correlation to the life you are living. Dave Hall is an example of that reality. If you value what the Bible teaches and actually live according to its guidelines, you will do well. If not, I guarantee your life will fall short. No matter how successful you are in the world's terms, you will find your life lacking.

Only when you begin to understand your true human-ity and compare it to God's divinity do you see what life is all about—to live in his shadow, under his wings, under his authority. And the Bible is the key to that story. The Bible points you in the right direction, to the right person, toward your Savior. It gives you an eyewitness perspective on the life of Jesus and shows you step-by-step how to have a revolu-tionary relationship with him. But it is up to you to trust, obey, and act upon his guidance.

❖   ❖   ❖

Over the years, I have heard many people question the reli-ability of the Bible. "How could anything created by man be fully reliable?" they ask. Well, why don't we look at the evidence? Here are just a few of the many facts to consider before we dig deeper into the reality and implications of Scripture. After all, if this is to be our final authority, we'd better know where we stand on the issue.

Today we have in our possession more than 5,300 known Greek manuscripts of the New Testament, another 10,000 Latin Vulgates (early Latin versions of the Bible), and 9,300 other early versions. That means we have more than 24,000 manuscript copies of portions of the New Testament.[11] Compare that to many of the great historical records we hold in high regard today—such as Caesar's *The Gallic Wars*, Pliny the Younger's *Natural History*, or Thucydides' *History*—and their manuscript evidence pales in comparison. The early New Testament manuscripts, dating within a few short years of the originals, reflect a powerful degree of reliability and accuracy.

Numerous manuscripts supporting the reliability of the Old Testament are also in our possession today. They include the Dead Sea Scrolls (first discovered in 1947), and date back to 150 BC. Moreover, many of the events, people, places, and customs in the Old and New Testaments are confirmed by secular historians and scientists. Serious, secular, nonbelieving archaeologists agree that the Bible is a remarkably historical document. And new discoveries are continuing to prove its reliability today.

At one point, scientists believed the book of Daniel had to be false because it referred to a king no one had heard of—King Belshazzar. Then, archaeologists found evidence for the appointed king. At one point, agnostic scientists were sure the city of Jericho had never existed. Then they found evidence to the contrary. The same was proven true regarding the size of the city of Nineveh, located in present-day Iraq.

At one point, scholars, scientists, and archaeologists alike believed the entire book of Acts to be a product of second-hand misinformation. Sir William Ramsay, known to be one of the greatest archaeologists to have ever lived, painstakingly traveled through Asia Minor looking to refute the claims of the book of Acts once and for all. After months of work, he had no choice but to reverse his own tightly held beliefs and conclude that the book was not only written in the first century, but should be regarded as a truly trustworthy and reliable source. The list could go on and on.

Take any book with that sort of reputation, reliability, historical accuracy, and longevity, and wouldn't you think that any one of us should look pretty closely at what it has to say? I think we would be hard-pressed not to use it as our daily guidebook for living. Yet how many of us actually do?

◧　◧　◧

The authority of Scripture is one of the oldest and most discussed questions of humankind. Yet it always stands up to the test.

When I hear people questioning whether the Bible is God's Word, I can't help but wonder if their hang-up is their view of God, not of the Bible itself. Do they think God is too small? After all, if God is God, couldn't he write a book that is without error? Couldn't he oversee a feat such as that? Of course he could! And he has!

If God couldn't write a book that is perfect, then why should you or I trust such a God with our lives? We must accept the Bible as *his Word* and treat it as his valuable Word *every day.* Just as the apostle Paul teaches, "All Scripture is God-breathed and is useful for teaching, rebuking, correcting and training in righteousness, so that the man of God may be thoroughly equipped for every good work" (2 Timothy 3:16-17, NIV).

For me, the evidence is too overwhelming to ignore, and the implications are astounding. The Bible is God's Word. And time in his Word is fundamental to true transformation. It's as simple as that. I urge you to give the Bible—God's Word to the human race—a chance to speak to you personally.

There are several books on the *New York Times* Best Sellers List right now that people will tell you transformed their lives. Whether a self-help book, a parenting manual, novel, or biography—the written word has the power to impact lives, and it has done so for centuries. So why is it so absurd to believe the same reality with the Bible? Why should we give any other book more credit?

I will tell you right now—with unwavering conviction— the Bible has the power to transform individuals in radical ways. I have seen it, and I know it personally. And let me tell you, it puts any other best seller to shame.

You can read all the self-help books you want. You can read the greats—the best philosophers over the centuries. But none will be as powerful or foundational as the Bible. It truly is *the* manual for life. And it stands as our greatest authority and guide because it points us to our greatest authority and guide, Jesus Christ.

To grow in your knowledge of God, to walk with him, to enjoy companionship with him, to be used by him—you have to pay attention to the Holy Word of God, the Bible. And please, don't rely on others to quote it—or *misquote* it—on your behalf. You must read it for yourself. You must believe it. And you must obey it. Then enjoy all it has to offer! Its content truly is staggering!

Maybe it's time to dust off that Good Book sitting on your nightstand. Maybe it's time to really dig in, carve out some time, and see what God wants to teach you. You're sure to find riches in its pages if you just give it time. And if you don't know where to turn, here are two suggestions:

- *The book of Proverbs.* With thirty-one chapters—one chapter for each day of the month—this book is a perfect addition to any daily reading. My dad taught me this when I was just a small boy. I've been following his leading ever since. Proverbs talks about every imaginable basic aspect of life—love, parenting, money, sex, God, relationships. It instructs on business, public policy, government, and family. It's the best counsel in the whole world. And it's free!
- *The Gospel of John.* This is the clearest and most spiritually fundamental book of the Bible, in my

mind. It was written by one of Jesus' closest disciples, a man who walked with him for his entire ministry. John clearly understood who Jesus is and what he has to offer. John's perspective in this Gospel is unique and powerful and will challenge your life on a daily basis. His object is clear, and it will deeply speak to you every time you read it seriously.

If you become an expert in these two books, practicing on a daily basis what they teach, you will be on your way to becoming a champion of the faith, I promise. Sure, it will take time. And yes, you will have frustrating days. Don't forget, we live in a broken world. Nothing will be perfect. But please, take heart. There is hope to be found in the Bible.

If, after searching the Scriptures yourself, you're still struggling, ask the pastor of a truly Bible-believing church in your area for help. Get into a Bible study with friends. Find others who will begin guiding you, reading the Bible with you, and showing you what it looks like to study God's Word on a daily basis. Set aside your pride and humbly ask for help. Ask God to guide you as you read it. Give it time to sink in. Memorize portions of it. Do what it says. (Jesus said in John 14:15, "If you love me, obey my commandments.") And then watch it do its work. It is the Word of God and the power of God! What more do you need?

7

BEAUTY FROM ASHES

In 1996, HUNDREDS of churches in a major South American city invited me to hold an evangelistic initiative there. As was the case with all our campaigns, it included months of planning, a strategic focus on training, and evangelistic preaching to as many people as possible. We worked with the local leaders for several months, planning the specific strategy. Thousands of individuals had already been trained to use the festival and surrounding events to reach out to their friends and neighbors. Television and radio advertisements saturated the airwaves. Buses and billboards carried the message across the city. And the news media were clamoring for interviews and insight. But during the week leading up to the actual festival, I focused my attention on hosting a live call-in television talk show program. It was something I had come to love. We aired the program across the region on as many networks as we could, and I spent an hour or more each night answering spiritual questions from struggling individuals. The program, *Night Talk with Luis Palau*, had become somewhat of a staple in our campaigns, and the inquiries and calls always proved to be intriguing.

None of the programming was scripted. It was just me, a telephone, a Bible, and a television camera. I took the calls, answered the questions as best I could, and pointed the callers back to their Savior, Jesus Christ. It wasn't complicated, but it was messy at times.

People called in with the oddest questions and the most serious concerns. It got to a point where I wasn't surprised by anything. People called in and poured out their hearts, right there on prime-time television with thousands of viewers. They told of suicidal thoughts, infidelity, addictions, and their blatant, ugly sins.

On one particular night, we didn't have much time left on the program. I had taken calls for nearly an hour, answering questions from a number of interesting characters. I was exhausted—emotionally and physically. But the second I heard the woman's voice, I knew this call would be different.

To protect her privacy, I will call her Ingrid.

"Luis, I need your counsel," she said in a soft, unassuming voice. "I'm twenty years old and I've done bad things. I'm having sex with married men. I can't stop. I don't want to stop.

But this is what my life has come to. I've been reading your book *Sex and Youth*, and I know what I'm doing is wrong. But I just can't find the strength or desire to change."

Her story unraveled from there.

She admitted having sex with several married men. She enjoyed it. And she especially loved the closeness.

"But these men don't love you," I told her. "They only want to use you. If you stay on this path, Ingrid, you will end up a bitter forty-year-old woman with tons of men in your past but no one in your present. You need to give them up."

"But they like me," she insisted.

"Do they want to marry you?"

"No."

"That's right. They just want to use you."

I could tell I wasn't convincing her. She seemed to be pulling away.

"I like to wear short skirts," she said, somewhat out of the blue. "I like to look cute. But people tell me I'm just asking for trouble." She seemed to be looking for excuses. I figured I should dig a little deeper.

"Tell me about your family," I said. "What about your parents? What do they think of all this?"

Immediately, I could tell I had hit a nerve. And I knew she was trying her best to hold back the tears.

"I don't have a family," she said softly. "My mom gave me away when I was five years old."

She couldn't hold back the tears any longer. Between sobs, the whole sad story came pouring out. Her mother had abandoned her. She didn't know her father. Her adoptive family was abusive. Her brothers took advantage of her sexually. And the repeated rapes finally left her detached, angry, and searching for love in other men. By the age of eighteen, she was sexually active with a number of older men. But her lifestyle was now taking its toll.

"You're not happy, Ingrid. Are you?"

Her crying kept her from responding.

"Ingrid, you need a change of heart. You need Jesus. He offers forgiveness. He wants to give you new life."

I could tell she was still fighting it.

"Ingrid," I said in the most caring voice I could muster, "the Bible says in Psalm 27:10, 'Even if my father and mother abandon me, the LORD will hold me close.' Your parents may have abandoned you, but Jesus will not. He *has* not! You're looking for real love, but you won't find it with these men. You won't find it in this world. You'll only find it with God."

My heart broke for this young woman.

"Ingrid, Jesus can make you a new woman," I told her. "He can clean you. He can change you . . . if you want him to. God has a plan for you, and you're not an accident. It's still God's purpose that you are here. It's not the worst thing that could have happened; the worst thing is never to have been born and never to have known this life. You can find meaning and purpose and direction through Christ, Ingrid. You can leave the past behind. Ugly as they may be, the experiences you've had are as nothing when compared to what's coming up if you choose to walk with the Lord. You can really turn your life around and make it into something beautiful and redemptive."

I couldn't tell if her silence was a sign of conviction or apathy.

I pleaded with her to let Jesus Christ into her life—to let him cleanse her and make her a new person. I challenged her as best I could, and I left the decision in her hands.

That's when she truly accepted Jesus Christ for who he is—the Lord and protector of her life. Live on television, I led her in a prayer of repentance and forgiveness. Ingrid tearfully prayed to Jesus, acknowledging who he was, asking him to be the Lord of her life.

At that, we parted ways. I hung up the phone and continued with the program, wondering if I would ever hear from Ingrid again. I had challenged her to come to our campaign that weekend—to meet face-to-face. She told me she would, but I had my doubts.

The next day, however, there she was. True to her word, she followed through and joined us. And that's when her story began to change.

A young woman standing next to her that night discovered that Ingrid lived near her church, and she invited Ingrid to attend the following Sunday. Again, Ingrid followed through and joined the lady at church. From there, the pastor of the church stepped in and connected Ingrid to another mature, single Christian lady who began to disciple her. Sensing the growth in her life, the church sent Ingrid to summer Bible camp where she was strengthened. She returned from camp, joined a group of young women in Bible study, was baptized, and began to grow even more.

The last time my wife and I saw Ingrid was in 2006, ten years after our first conversation over the phone. We were holding a similar campaign in a Central American nation, and I was told that a young lady in the area wanted to greet my wife and me. The second I heard her name, I knew exactly who it was. I hadn't forgotten our conversation.

Ingrid had grown into a beautiful, mature woman. She had left her job for full-time Christian work and was now serving God as a missionary, leading people to Jesus Christ. She was doing amazingly well—still walking with the Lord and being used by him in mighty ways.

When we sat down to speak with her, it was as if I were talking with a completely different person from the young woman who had called in to our broadcast. She was so happy—so fulfilled. And her contentment was clear. She had found her purpose. She had found healing. She had found life.

As I left our meeting, Psalm 113 echoed in my mind:

Praise the LORD!
Praise, O servants of the LORD,
     praise the name of the LORD!

Blessed be the name of the LORD
     from this time forth and forevermore!
From the rising of the sun to its setting,
     the name of the LORD is to be praised!

> *The LORD is high above all nations,*
>   *and his glory above the heavens!*
> *Who is like the LORD our God,*
>   *who is seated on high,*
> *who looks far down*
>   *on the heavens and the earth?*
> *He raises the poor from the dust*
>   *and lifts the needy from the ash heap,*
> *to make them sit with princes,*
>   *with the princes of his people.*[12]

That, my friend, is revolutionary—ashes into beauty. That is the power of Jesus Christ.

I don't think I've ever heard anyone call me *beautiful*, but I have seen the same reality of being raised from the ashes played out in my life. I have tasted the dust. I have experienced the pain. I have seen the beauty on the other side. And I've learned a few things along the way, things that just might change your life for the better as well.

If we've lived for any length of time, we've all faced our fair share of pain and heartache. We've all gone through difficult stretches. We've all dealt with difficult circumstances, some more severe than others. And we're always one step away from despair. But we can't forget that we're also just one step away from *victory*. It all depends on what we do with our plight.

Though your life may not contain the same graphic elements as Ingrid's, you have your own story, and it probably has some pain associated with it. The questions, the loneliness, and the struggles are there. And perhaps you've been wondering how to get out of it.

Like Ingrid, you have a choice. You can choose to live in the pain—to experience it and relive it daily. Or you can choose to rise above it. I know which one God wants for you. After all, he is in the business of raising people from the dead and lifting individuals from the dust. But he lets you choose.

The Bible says, "God has given us everything we need for living a godly life." Why? To "enable you to share his divine nature and escape the world's corruption caused by human desires" (2 Peter 1:3-4). God has given us what we need so that we can *overcome*—so that we can find victory!

In view of all this, make every effort to respond to God's promises. Supplement your faith with a generous provision of moral excellence, and moral excellence with knowledge, and knowledge with self-control, and self-control with patient endurance, and patient endurance with godliness, and godliness with brotherly affection, and brotherly affection with love for everyone.

The more you grow like this, the more productive and useful you will be in your knowledge of our Lord Jesus Christ. But those who fail to develop

in this way are shortsighted or blind, forgetting that
they have been cleansed from their old sins.

So, dear brothers and sisters, work hard to prove
that you really are among those God has called and
chosen. Do these things, and you will never fall
away. Then God will give you a grand entrance into
the eternal Kingdom of our Lord and Savior Jesus
Christ. (2 Peter 1:5-11)

Don't be shortsighted. Our citizenship is in heaven. Our goal
is eternity. You are among those whom God has called and
chosen. And your desire is a grand entrance into the eternal
Kingdom of your Lord.

Like Ingrid, you have the ability to rise above any obstacle.
No matter your background, your pain, or your trials, you can
rise above them. God has promised it. Now you just need to
believe it and act on it.

8

WHAT THE BIBLE SAYS ABOUT YOU

IT WAS BONE COLD and pitch-dark on the snowy mountain. For more than eight hours, rescue teams and volunteers had been scouring the countryside, looking for a nine-year-old boy named Dominic. The temperature had dropped further than anticipated, and the searchers knew that a small child would not survive long in those conditions.

Dominic and his father had been separated late in the day, mistakenly taking separate ski lifts up the mountain. The weather was now turning bad, and the outlook was not optimistic. The local authorities had rounded up more than ninety volunteers to look for the young boy, but they were getting cold and tired, and they were losing hope.

"Given the condition of our volunteers," said one of the rescue workers, "I can't imagine the state of little Dominic."

With each passing hour, as the volunteers' pace slowed and their demeanor grew more somber, Dominic's mother grew more frantic. By dawn, they still had found no trace of the boy.

With the coming of daylight, two helicopters joined the search, and within fifteen minutes hope was rekindled. One of the helicopter pilots spotted ski tracks well off the beaten path and radioed the location to the crews on the ground. Volunteers on foot quickly headed in that direction as the pilot did his best to follow the trail. The ground team finally connected with the tracks, which led to a pair of skis propped up in the snow. From there, the tracks changed to small footprints, which led into an evergreen forest and ended near a large tree with a cluster of boughs at its base. Amid the branches, they saw glimpses of what appeared to be a brightly colored ski parka—the same color Dominic had been wearing when he disappeared. But there was no movement and no sound.

The rescue workers held their breath, bracing for the worst. After all, the young boy had spent the entire night on the cold mountain, with no preparation or planning. But as they drew closer, Dominic's head popped above the branches. He was alive and doing well!

Dominic shivered from the cold as the rescuers quickly pulled him to safety, wrapped him in blankets, and raced down the mountainside to where an emergency medical team was waiting to check his condition. To everyone's surprise, little Dominic was in perfect shape. "He's doing great," the head of the mountain rescue patrol announced. "In fact, he's in better shape than we are right now."

As the story unfolded, it became clear why Dominic had fared so well. Quite simply, he had followed his father's instructions. Knowing the possibility of danger in the outdoors, Dominic's father had the forethought to warn his young son and give him lifesaving tools, in case he lost his way.

"If you get lost," he had told his son early the prior day, "get to safety, find a tree, and cover yourself in branches. Most important of all, once you're there . . . *don't move!*"

The little boy had trusted his father enough to do exactly what he'd been told. So when the unthinkable happened . . . when he looked up and found himself lost and alone . . . he knew what to do. Little Dominic—in the midst of his tears and unthinkable fear—began skiing toward a large tree in the distance. More than one hundred yards from the tree, the snow became thick and the slope worked against him, so he ditched his skis and hiked the rest of the way. Coming to the tree, he dug deep into the snow, snuggled up next to the trunk, and covered himself in branches. And then he stayed put.

As the night drew on and the cold did its best to penetrate his clothes, Dominic kept the faith, trusting that his father's guidance would keep him safe.

You can imagine that little Dominic would never have thought of all that on his own. He had not taken a formal survival class. He didn't have the proper instincts that would allow him to figure out what to do without prompting. He simply obeyed his wise and loving father. And why not?

Had Dominic taken matters into his own hands—had he decided that he didn't like following rules, or he didn't like trees, or he just thought it was more fun to stay out in the snow—the story would have turned out much differently. Yet how often do we try to take control of our life's situation and do what we think feels right?

Dominic was hailed for his courage and strength. The news media told how smart and how brave he was. But in life we often look at things another way.

Sure, you could say those rules his father gave him were just guidelines. They were just good suggestions. Follow them or don't, it's up to you, little Dominic. Do what feels good to you. But I guarantee you, if Dominic had decided not to follow those rules, if he had decided to do things his own way, he wouldn't have survived that night on the mountain.

The same principle applies to our ability to survive in this world without paying heed to God's wisdom as revealed in the Bible. So often, we hold to our individuality at the utter expense of our safety. We celebrate our freedom. We revel in our ability to do what we want—until reality hits.

Sure, we could look at God's principles for living as just a bunch of boring rules. We could look at the Bible as an annoying "buzz kill," designed to take away our fun. Or we can look at it the way Dominic did with his father's instructions—as hard-and-fast principles, from a loving Father, that will save our lives. After all, we can't kid ourselves. Left to our own devices, we get into trouble on a regular basis. We make mistakes and end up in hot water more than we want to admit. (Or is it just me who does that?) When I find myself in those places, I sure am glad I have someone guiding me through the rubble to safety on the other side—someone who knows me deeply, who knows my needs, and who wants what is best for me.

I've been blessed by walking daily with my heavenly Father for the past sixty years as a believer. And I have found that his Word truly is "a lamp to guide my feet and a light for my path" (Psalm 119:105).

If you take the time to study the Bible, you might be surprised by what it says about you specifically. Its instructions for living are far more clear and comprehensive than the instructions given by Dominic's father, and they go into far more detail than even a good Eagle Scout survival manual.

I still vividly remember the day when the power of the Bible truly struck home for me. I was twelve years old and away at a two-week summer camp in the beautiful Sierra of central Argentina. It was our last night in the mountains, the sun was just setting on the surrounding peaks, and I was completely panicked. I knew what was coming.

Every night for the past week, our counselor, Frank Chandler, had come to our tent at lights-out—with a Bible in one hand and a flashlight in the other—and called one of the boys outside to talk. It wasn't long—no more than ten minutes at a time. But it was important. And clearly, it was serious.

Each night, as the boy returned to the tent, those of us who hadn't been called yet would pump him for information. What was it all about? Why was it so important?

By this final evening, I had put enough of the puzzle pieces together to have an idea of what was in store. I knew the conversation had to do with the Bible, my life, and Jesus. But the details would have to wait for my own conversation, which I knew was quickly looming. I was terrified. For some reason, the last thing I wanted to do was have a conversation about God.

I was nearly in a sweat by the time Frank came to the tent. I pretended I was asleep, thinking he would go away. It didn't work. Frank was determined.

"Come on, Palau," he said, "get up."

I quickly figured out I couldn't put one past him (especially after he flipped my cot and dumped me on the ground). I grabbed my flashlight and headed outside, my head slung deep between my shoulders and a scowl on my face.

Outside, the air was muggy. Although the heat of the summer in the Sierra was somewhat cooler than in the hot city, it still was overwhelming.

As we began to walk, I could sense the weather turning. The wind was picking up and occasional raindrops began to fall. But Frank would not be deterred by a little rain. We found a fallen tree that offered some shelter and sat down. Before I could gather my wits, Frank began to speak.

"Luis," he said sharply. "Are you a Christian, or not?"

I was somewhat surprised by the question. It was so

blunt and seemed so insensitive. Frank knew I came from a Christian family. He knew I could say the right words and sing all the right songs. But he also knew my attitude. He had heard my nasty tongue. He had dealt with my bursts of anger. He wasn't convinced that I truly knew Jesus Christ for myself. And to tell you the truth, I wasn't sure either. In fact, I was pretty certain I was going to hell. I hadn't committed any *big* sins—I hadn't murdered anyone or stolen anything, and drugs and alcohol were not a part of my young life—but I knew in my heart I was a sinner.

I finally answered after a long pause, "I don't think I'm a Christian."

Frank wasted no time responding. After all, it was beginning to rain. "Well, it's not a matter of whether you *think* so. Are you or aren't you?" (He was harsh, which is not a technique I would recommend, but it worked for me.)

"No," I replied. "I'm pretty sure I'm not."

That's when he pulled out his Bible—a worn-out, well-read, leather-bound book. He turned to the book of Romans.

"Luis," he said, "I want you to listen to this." At that, he began reading aloud:

"If you confess with your lips, Luis, that Jesus is Lord, Luis, and believe in your heart, Luis, that God raised him from the dead . . . then you, Luis, will be saved. For man believes with his heart and so is justified, and he confesses with his lips and so is saved" (Romans 10:9-10, RSV, adapted).

Me? Luis? I thought. *Did it really say that? Was it really talking about me?*

I was stunned. I found myself looking over Frank's shoulder, half expecting to see my name on the pages of his Bible. *Me! This book has something to do with me!*

That conversation proved to be the most important of my entire life. That was when I committed my life fully to Jesus Christ. Frank led me in a prayer that set me on an entirely new path. It changed my heart, took away much of my pain, and gave me a renewed purpose. That was when I truly became a Christian. I will never forget that night—February 14, 1947.

That was more than sixty years ago, but I still remember it as if it were yesterday. That was the first time I realized that God actually cared about me. That night, I learned that the Bible—the old book that Frank held in his hand—was written for me!

I know that sounds conceited, but it's true. And it's true for you, as well. God designed each of us with a unique purpose. He created you and me, specifically, because he wanted to, because he cares for us, and because he wants us to spend eternity with him (Jeremiah 1:4-5). In fact, he cares for us so much that when we messed up the plans—when we broke ties with him—he gave up his only Son in order to restore our relationship.

◈　◈　◈

If you've been a Christian for any amount of time, the reality of God's love and purpose for you has been ingrained into your being. God cares deeply for you. The Bible was written specifically to you. It is God's love letter to you. So why does our spiritual journey seem so dry at times? Why does the Bible feel more like a textbook than a love letter? And why is it often so hard to get anything out of it? Could it be that you're still not quite sure this book was really, truly written for you? Could it be that you're still wondering about its relevance in your life?

The Bible has a lot to say about you. Not just about you as a human being, but you specifically—you personally. In fact, much of the Bible is devoted to telling you who you really are. Look at just a few examples:

- You were made in God's image. (Genesis 1:26-27)
- God wants what is best for you. (Jeremiah 29:11)
- You have the opportunity to be free from unnecessary burdens. (Matthew 11:28)
- God wants a relationship with you. (John 3:16)
- You have the opportunity to be free from oppression. (John 8:36)
- You are loved by your Creator! (John 16:27)
- You were created to be like God in true righteousness and holiness. (Ephesians 4:24)
- God cares about you. (1 Peter 5:7)
- God forgives every sin, if you confess it from your heart. (1 John 1:9)
- God loves you. (1 John 4:19)

I could go on and on, but these few examples give you a taste. When you really dig in and read, it's actually quite staggering. The Bible talks about your formation, your maturation, your exploration—even your life experience. Sure, you might not find your name in the pages of the Bible—my counselor, Frank, added that for dramatic effect—but your DNA, your makeup, clearly is. (Many Christians don't even realize the power of this.) Here are a few more things the Bible says about you:

- You were created as a unique person. (Psalm 139:13-16)
- You long for truth. (Matthew 5:6)
- You were made for love. (Matthew 22:37-39)
- You were made to be part of something bigger than yourself. (1 Corinthians 12:27)
- You were made for adventure. (2 Corinthians 2:14)
- You desire freedom. (Galatians 5:1)
- You were made for knowledge. (2 Peter 1:5)
- You were made for relationships. (1 John 4:19)

Does that sound like you? Does it have the ring of truth? To me, it sure sounds like the Bible knows what it's talking about. But it doesn't end there. Look at some of the promises it offers for those who believe:

- The spiritually dead will become alive. (Isaiah 26:19; John 3:1-7)
- The blind will see. (Isaiah 35:5; Matthew 11:4-5)

- The guilty will be forgiven. (Mark 11:25; Luke 6:27-36; John 3:16-17)
- The empty will be filled. (Luke 1:6-25)
- The lost will be found. (Luke 15)
- The slave will be set free. (Acts 16:25-34; Romans 6)
- The cursed will be redeemed. (Galatians 3:13)
- The condemned will be exonerated. (Colossians 2:13-15)
- The hopeless will be filled with hopeful expectation. (Hebrews 6:19)
- The beggar will become a child of the king. (James 1:9)

For me, that's staggering! This Bible—written thousands of years ago—actually gives me worth, purpose, importance, and a pretty exciting future. *It was written for me!* It's not just a book of suggestions or observations about life. It's not just an intriguing story written for entertainment. It's not just something to read on an occasional basis, something that merely helps me "live a better life."

The Bible teaches me that I matter and that someone cares for me. As a matter of fact, that someone is no less than the creator of the world, our heavenly Father! (Read Psalm 19 and Psalm 119.)

That gives me hope. That gives me worth. And it makes me want to read more! What about you?

Doesn't the idea of having a heavenly Father sound appealing? Don't you want—and need—someone you can truly depend on? Someone who will show you the way . . .

who will guide you . . . who will look out for you? Don't you want that?

I know of many grown men and women who have never felt accepted, appreciated, or loved by their earthly fathers. They go their entire lives hoping to hear "I love you" or "I care about you" or "I am so proud of you" from their fathers, but they have been left wanting. Whether the father was in the home yet emotionally detached, or whether he took off years ago, the pain he caused and the injustice he inflicted is substantial. Even worse, he ruined his children's view of God.

More and more, I'm hearing young boys and girls talk the same way, sharing stories about abandonment, guilt, confusion, and fear, not to mention outright abuse—all of it stemming from absent fathers. Therapists and counselors can attest to the pain these children feel.

I recently talked with a teenage girl who was in counseling for cutting her wrists. You might wonder where such despair comes from. But she knows. It comes from the rejection and pain inflicted by her absent father. She's so lonely. She's in so much pain.

We are living in a generation of fatherless individuals, and the fallout is enormous. Naturally, for people struggling with abandonment issues, to think of a father that loves them is a rather odd idea—a foreign concept. If that's how you feel, please know that you're not alone. We all have an innate desire to be accepted and loved by our fathers. It's ingrained in us. It was placed there by our heavenly Father.

I have struggled at times with this same issue. My own father left when I was just ten years old. Sure, it wasn't his choice; he died. But nonetheless, I grew up without a father. I was robbed of the opportunity to know and be loved by my dad. And for years I have struggled with this question: *What does it really mean to have a father who loves you?*

❖ ❖ ❖

Ray, another friend of mine, grew up with a similar longing. No father. No guidance. No protection. His solution, though, was nothing any parents would want for their young son.

When Ray first told me his story, I was appalled. He called in to one of my live television programs one evening in El Paso, Texas. He was sixteen years old and active in a gang. They called themselves the Fatherless Gang, and they were four hundred members strong. Ray had no desire to be in a gang. It wasn't as if he was a troublemaker or rabble-rouser. But he longed for family. He longed for protection. He needed a father. So did all the other boys. So they formed a gang. They created their own family, and they offered protection to one another—from bullies at school or on the streets. They did what their fathers were not there to do.

At first, I thought this gang might be a unique anomaly in the fabric of our family-friendly society. But I quickly learned how wrong I was. The fact is, nearly half the kids in the United States don't have their father in the home. The statistics grow even higher when you include Europe or

Latin America. And the implications for social stability are astounding.

For kids like Ray, the lack of a father eats them up. It consumes their minds. Even the word *father* raises feelings of anger, resentment, and fear.

I don't want that pain for anyone. And no one has to live that way. The fact is that we each have a Father who cares for us. You have a heavenly Father who loves you and who wants a relationship with you. Not only is he interested in you, he is completely focused on you. He is never too busy for you. He will never take off and leave you. He will never disappoint you. He will never make a promise he can't keep. He will never go back on his word. He will never hurt you, will never demean you, will never make fun of you, and will never cut you down. He cares for you deeply. God is our Father!

I realize that many people already *know* this in their minds. But it's one thing to *know* it and another to actually live in it—to actually let it sink in and enjoy it—to actually experience our heavenly Father's love. After all, God has a lot to say about you. He has a lot to say *to* you. And his promises have a profound impact *on* you. He wants a relationship with you.

But what's the key to making this relationship with your heavenly Father real? How can you take it from an appealing idea to a powerful reality?

The key is Jesus Christ, our Savior and Lord.

The Bible tells us that "no one truly knows the Father except the Son [Jesus Christ] and those to whom the Son chooses to reveal him" (Matthew 11:27). In John 14:6, Jesus says, "I am the way, the truth, and the life. No one can come to the Father except through me."

Our access to the Father is through Jesus Christ and Jesus Christ alone. And our true understanding of who the Father is comes through Jesus as well. It's nothing we can conjure up on our own. It must come through God's Son. He must do the work in our hearts. He must transform our thinking and clear out the space for us to truly experience a powerful relationship with God.

The only way you can make your relationship with your heavenly Father real is to draw closer to Jesus. The more you trust him—the more you understand his true nature, his teaching, and his expectations for your life—the more you will find closeness with your true and loving Father. There is no other way. There is no other path.

Come close to Jesus. As you do, you will come close to God.

9

THE IMAGE OF GOD

THE RECOVERY WING of the hospital was dark and quiet. It was a weeknight, past most people's bedtime. My wife, Patricia, was recovering from cancer surgery and she couldn't sleep. I flipped through the television channels, doing my best to keep her company. It had been a rough ordeal, and several more months of chemotherapy and recovery still lay ahead. It wouldn't be easy.

That evening, the entire floor was quiet. The nurses had finally left us alone for a while. It was just the two of us—and our thoughts and fears. As my beautiful Patricia sat in bed— sick, exhausted, and weak—she shared her heart with me.

"You know," she said as the television flickered quietly in

the background, "I have never been more convinced of the reality of body, soul, and spirit."

It was an odd conversation starter, but I'm always up for a good theological discussion. Intrigued, I responded, "Really? Why?"

"Here I sit, my physical body broken, sick, and in pain," she explained. "My soul—my emotions—are up and down. Some days are good—full of cheer. Some days bad—full of tears. But then, clearer than ever before, I am aware of my spirit. No matter the day—good or bad—I have an overwhelming sense of peace. It is deeper than my emotions, and far more profound than my physical body. The only explanation is that it's my spirit, indwelt by and surrendered to Jesus Christ."

As I looked back on the previous several months, I could see it too. Throughout the entire process, Patricia had been an amazing example for me. Joy, peace, and acceptance reigned over her life. Sure, it was difficult and painful. And of course she would fight for complete healing with every ounce of strength she had. But she knew the Lord was ultimately still on the throne. She had peace beyond understanding. And she was okay with whatever the outcome. And why not? Paul the apostle tells us that Christ lives in us (Galatians 2:20) and that our body is the temple of God's Holy Spirit (1 Corinthians 6:19).

It reminded me of the day we found out about Patricia's cancer. We returned home from the hospital and I immediately retreated to my office downstairs. Overwhelmed by the news of the day, I began to weep. I cried my eyes out. I pleaded with the Lord. As the minutes went on and I was able to calm myself, I heard music playing in the distance. It was my wife, upstairs, at the piano.

As I sat there on my knees—broken, distraught, and completely perplexed—she was upstairs in the living room, praising the God she serves. The song? "It Is Well with My Soul."

That, my friend, is reality.

I have never had to deal with something as serious as cancer myself, but I have had my fair share of tough situations. And I can't help but agree with my wife. It is in those instances that I am most aware of my true, God-given nature. "But the person who is joined to the Lord is one spirit with him" (1 Corinthians 6:17). It doesn't make the situation easier, but it does give us hope in the midst of it. For it is in our weakness that God proves himself strong. It is when we come to the end of ourselves, when we are forced to trust in God alone, that we finally realize the power and peace he has to offer—a peace the world cannot supply (John 14:27).

I may never handle a situation with the same ease and understanding as my wife does. (I've always been more emotional.) But in the quietness of my heart, I can always recognize God's Spirit at work within me. I can always know he is working everything—even the bad stuff—together for my good because I love him and am called according to his purpose (Romans 8:28). That is one reality we all would do well to dwell upon when in the midst of difficult times.

According to the Bible, you were made in the image of God. You were created in his likeness. But what does that really mean? And what is this "spirit" that joins us together?

Like God himself, you are a triune being. Triune means three in one: body, soul, and spirit. Does that seem odd? It's not, really.

Your being consists of three main parts. The first is your physical body. This is the means by which you interact with the physical world. You are able to touch, taste, smell, hear, and see.

You feel physical pain and physical pleasure. You can function: walk, run, eat, and talk. Your physical being is what ties you to creation. Your physical body is confined to this world, and it is very fragile—one breath or one heartbeat away from death.

Then there is your soul. This encompasses your emotions, will, and intellect. It includes your personality. It is what makes you human. It is how you interact with others—how you process your existence in the world. It is how you experience life on a deeper level. Your soul allows you to have meaningful relationships. It gives you the ability to love and hate, to be happy and angry. It gives you the capacity to make decisions, to be rational. Without a soul, you would be carnal, impersonal, and purely physical. With it, your life is drastically different—at least it should be.

Many people seem to believe body and soul are the complete equation. Nothing more. I don't buy it. If that were true, our lives would be cursed. Sure, we might be happy for a time, but eventually everything fails. Relationships give way to conflict. Wives grow weary of their husbands, and vice versa. Children grow tired of their parents. Friendships become strained and distant. We give up, withdraw, and look for greener pastures on another hill. (Does that sound familiar?)

But that is not all there is—praise God! By his grace, he designed us—you and me—to be in relationship with him. It's why he gave us the Bible and why he sent his Son. And it's why he gave us a third key component to our being—the part we call *spirit*. This is what allows us to be connected to our Creator and to our Savior. It is what allows us to truly know God.

The human spirit is what separates us from the rest of creation. It is what makes us unique—potential children of God (John 1:12).

That's right; you are unique!

If you have trouble believing you have a unique spirit, don't worry. Many religious leaders have trouble believing it as well. They would like to explain it away or lump it in as just another aspect of the soul. But the human spirit is real. It is unique. It is different from the soul in that it connects us to God. Sadly, a majority of the world's population lives as if the spirit were dead. And, apart from God . . . it is.

Think of your spirit in terms of a lightbulb. You can have a fully intact, fully functional lightbulb—something that looks perfect and complete on the outside. Yet, if it's not plugged into a power source, or if the electric current has been cut off, you won't see an essential element of the lightbulb. Apart from a proper connection to a power source, it's difficult to comprehend the purpose of a lightbulb. You might admire its aesthetic (physical) properties, but it won't take long to realize that something is missing. Clearly, the lightbulb isn't living up to its full potential.

The apostle Paul put it this way: "As for you, you were dead in your transgressions and sins, in which you used to live when you followed the ways of this world" (Ephesians 2:1-2, NIV). Apart from God, we're disconnected from the power source that brings forth and reveals our full potential—and our intended purpose.

Such is life for many in our world.

◈   ◈   ◈

Deep down, we all know there is more to life than mere physical existence. A while back, I spent some time in the Scottish Highlands. It's a beautiful area, full of history and legend. The countryside is littered with castles, ruins, battlegrounds, and memorials to fallen heroes. I have had the opportunity to visit a number of the popular castles over the years. I have even visited some of the more private and exclusive ones as well.

It seems that every castle has its story of paranormal activity—a ghost or spirit that is said to haunt its halls. It's creepy, to say the least. The tour guides or locals tell stories of children wandering the corridors, an old lady who spends her time in the chapel, or card-playing servants making noise into the wee hours of the night.

Why is it that ghost stories make the hair on the back of our necks stand up? Why is it that tales of ghosts and spirits make us think twice about reality? Because deep down we know there is more to this life than what we can see. We know there is much more to reality than the physical world. Even kids can sense it.

An old mentor of mine, pastor Ray Stedman, once told me a story about one of his daughters. One morning, as Ray lay asleep, his young daughter bounded into the room and crawled into bed with him. Though now fully awake, Ray thought it would be funny to pretend to stay asleep, no matter what she did. As she jumped and hollered, poked and punched, he lay quietly, trying not to move or make a peep. Finally, his daughter crawled up and sat right on his chest. Reaching down, she pried open one of his eyelids and whispered, "Are you in there, Daddy?"

It's a silly story, I know. But to me, it strikes a chord. Even small children know there is more to life than our physical bodies. Even children know our true being is more than skin-deep. It's a reality we can't deny.

I recently went to the funeral of an old friend. As in many cases, the body was prepared and presented, lying in an open casket at the front of the church. With makeup caked across my old friend's face, the morticians had done their best to make his body look as if nothing were wrong—just a peaceful sleep. But it didn't take a rocket scientist to realize there was something wrong. As I stood there, staring at my friend, I couldn't help but realize that it was not him. He wasn't there anymore.

My friend's body lay peacefully—for a time. Soon enough, it would decay and the physical would disappear. But his soul and his spirit—the real person—were still intact and very much alive. They had clearly departed to another place. I knew without a doubt where my friend had gone. Those who believe in Jesus Christ, the Son of God, have the joy of entering immediately into heaven (2 Corinthians 5:8).

You may be thinking, "This is all great, Luis. Christianity 101. But even if I do believe, even if I say it all makes sense, how does it really change my life right now? How is any of this relevant to me as I struggle through the rat race of life? I have kids. I have bills. I have a nagging spouse. I have a boss I don't trust. I have a life I don't enjoy. I never get enough sleep. I'm not happy—I'm exhausted."

You don't have to wait for heaven to experience a great, revolutionary life. You can have it here and now. It is real. It is tangible. And it is spectacular.

◙　　◙　　◙

Like flipping a light switch, it doesn't take much to transform your life. The action is really quite simple, though it represents a deeper, more complex reality. When you surrender your life to Jesus Christ, you plug in to a source of infinite power—power that is more than sufficient to change your life completely. On the other hand, if left unconnected—as you may have already discovered—life can get pretty desperate. I've seen it far too often, even in the nicest of people.

So how do you flip the switch? How do you plug into the right power source? How do you reach your full potential? It's quite simple: You turn away from yourself and turn toward God.

When you want to turn on a lamp in a room, you don't concern yourself with the lightbulb. Instead, you focus on the switch. To turn on a light, you don't ask it to please turn on. You don't rub it or chant to it. You don't do anything to the bulb. Instead, you turn your attention to the source of power and deal with it there. And so it is with your spiritual life.

So often we are tempted to focus on ourselves when we discuss or ponder our spiritual lives. We wonder if we've done enough, if we're good enough, or if we know enough. But quite frankly, that's not what matters. That's not where our focus should be. After all, no one has done enough. No one is good enough (Romans 3:23).

If we want to reach our full potential, we need to go to the source—we need to turn to God—in every situation. We need to look to him for power, not to ourselves.

As much as we try, life is too difficult to tackle on our own. When we take on the trials of the world—which are bound to come—we need more than our own minds and willpower to make it through. We need help from above! But so often it's hard to let go of the anxieties of life and let God take over. It's hard for us to take our focus off the lightbulb and turn to the source. But when we finally do, our lives begin to work the way they were intended. It's not a coincidence. It's a biblical truth! God commands us to cast all our cares on him (1 Peter 5:7) and to have confidence in him (Proverbs 3:26). The result? "Then you will go on your way in safety, and your foot will not stumble; when you lie down, you will not be afraid; when you lie down, your sleep will be sweet" (Proverbs 3:23-24, NIV). That's quite a promise!

Think about it—the wisdom that created the earth's foundation and the knowledge that set the heavens in motion are available to us through Jesus Christ. When we tap into his source, we receive his gifts—sound judgment, discernment, grace, safety, and security. But most important, when we trust in the Lord, he pours out his wisdom on us. He gives us the strength and guidance to love our neighbors, to live righteously, and to humbly follow him.

We are the light of the world (Matthew 5:14). We are called to shine brightly. But like any good light, the only way we can accomplish that task is to be plugged in and focused on the right source.

Imagine what life would be like if millions of followers of Jesus Christ throughout the world actually lived out this biblical lifestyle. What a vast, transformational difference it would make!

10

EMMANUEL: GOD WITH US

In many of the northern provinces of Argentina, we still have several Model T Fords on our roads. I'm always amazed at the number. We call them Kick Fords because of the three kick pedals used to operate them. You kick one to go forward, another to go backward, and still another for the brake. Pretty basic.

I remember hearing a story several years ago about a young man with a Kick Ford. I haven't met him, so I can't confirm the story. But I love it nonetheless.

This young man was driving his antique Model T on a motorway near Detroit, Michigan. He had just fixed it up and was proud to have it out on the open road. But, of course, the second he got his speed up, the motor died. He kicked the pedal for neutral and let it coast to the side of the road. Discouraged and angry, he popped the hood and began to tinker with the motor. He tightened this and loosened that. He did whatever he could think of. (After all, he had just rebuilt the engine. You would imagine he would know what to do.) But it was all to no avail. The dirty black Kick Ford was immovable. That's when a shiny new Lincoln Continental pulled up behind him, parking along the motorway. Out stepped a respectable-looking older gentleman.

The man was dressed to the nines—tuxedo, top hat, shiny black shoes, and clean white gloves. He clearly was on his way to an important gala of some sort. As he approached the young man, he pulled off one of his white gloves and offered his hand. "It looks like you're having trouble, young man. What seems to be the problem?"

The young man was put off immediately. "What does it look like? It's dead."

He wasn't sure what this aristocrat thought he would be able to do.

"Do you mind if I help?" the older gentleman offered.

"I've got it," the young man said roughly. (He clearly did not.)

Graciously, the older man stepped back and watched as the young man's greasy hands tinkered with the motor. Several minutes passed.

"Are you sure you don't want my help?" the older gentleman offered again.

"No, I've got it."

Several more minutes passed with no progress or signs of life from the motor.

"Young man," the gentleman interjected again, "are you sure?"

The young man was fed up. Unable to diagnose the problem, he was tired of this old man's hounding. "Sure," he responded, defeated. "Take a look. I don't know what you expect to find."

At that, the older gentleman stepped forward, looked at the motor calmly, and turned to the boy. "Jump in and I'll tell you when to give it a start."

The young man climbed hesitantly into the cab and waited for the older man's instructions. Within seconds, he heard a call from the front of the car, "Start it up."

With one turn of the ignition switch, the engine fired to life.

The young man was in awe. He jumped out of the cab and excitedly approached the gentleman. "How did you know what to do?" he asked. "Who are you?"

Placing his top hat back on his head and carefully returning his white gloves to his hands, the gentleman responded with a sly smile, "Young man, I'm Henry Ford. I designed this thing. I knew what your problem was the second I saw it."

Who knows if that story is true? I'd like to believe it is. I can just picture Henry Ford reaching under the hood of that car—tinkering with his own creation. But either way, the picture is powerful. Many of us are like the young man with the broken Kick Ford sitting on the side of the motorway. We're trying desperately to fix our problems ourselves, yet we're failing miserably. And all along, our Creator is standing by and watching, waiting for us to hand over control. He's just waiting to be given his rightful authority. So why, like the young man, do we hesitate to give him a shot at fixing the problems in our lives?

Somewhere along the way, as we grow up, we learn to balk at authority, even though dependence on others, which we learn at a young age, is essential to our survival. I think most experts would agree that children thrive in a structured, discipline-oriented environment. (No, I'm not talking about baby boot camp.) But it's a fact that we flourish when we have guidelines, when we know what our boundaries are, and when we have authority figures directing us in the way we should go. Yet so often we live—or at least try to live—in ways that are in complete opposition to that reality. In our human relationships, we learn to "do life" on our own. We learn to trust ourselves and no one else. It's part of our survival instinct, I suppose. But in all honesty, we all want and need someone to guide us through the twists and turns of life.

As a young boy, I was under my father's authority. I lived under his protection and love. Frankly, it felt like true freedom. I knew I was taken care of. I knew I was valued. And I knew he would teach me how to truly live. (Praise God I had a father I could respect.) When he died, I lost that. I was separated from him. How I longed to have those days back again.

For most of my growing up years, I had no father to tell me how to survive—and I desperately missed his guidance. But by the grace of God, several men came into my life to fill that void. And the greatest of all was Jesus Christ. I have been living under his authority, protection, and love ever since.

◈　　◈　　◈

In the days following the tragic earthquake in Haiti in January 2010, stories began flooding news outlets around the world. Most were of despair, pain, and utter destruction. The images plastered on television sets and in newspapers were horrendous. The stories were heart wrenching. Children who had lost their parents. Parents who had lost their children. Kids being pulled bruised and broken from the rubble. Orphans struggling to get to adoptive parents. But as I watched the reports on Haiti—as I tried to process the pain and agony those people were facing—one story was seared into my memory. It has stuck with me ever since. It was the story of a young girl, Alyanah, and her loving father, Emmanuel.

The Sanson-Rejouis family had been living in Haiti for only eight months when the quake hit. The mother, Emily, a United Nations employee, was at work when the ground started to shake. Immediately knowing the severity of the disaster, she was desperate to get to her husband and three daughters, who were back at the hotel where they had been staying. When she arrived, she found the building reduced to a pile of rubble.

Devastated, yet still holding on to hope, Emily enlisted the help of rescue workers and locals to begin digging through the cinder blocks and debris. She was desperate, she was determined . . . and she thought she heard some signs of life coming from the ruins.

It was hours before the rescue workers were able to dig down to where they thought the father and children might be. When they finally found traces of the family, the results were heartbreaking and exhilarating at the same time. Under the debris, Emily found her husband, Emmanuel, dead from the crushing weight of the building. He was facedown, crouched beneath the rubble. But underneath his crumpled body lay Alyanah, the youngest daughter, very much alive and well. Aside from a broken leg, she had been saved from the disaster.

Piecing the story together over the following days, Emily came to realize what had happened during the quake. It left her broken and in awe. While most people scurried for safety, looking out for their own well-being, Emmanuel's first thoughts were of his children. Grabbing the closest and youngest child—Alyanah—he held her close as the quake struck, sheltering her body as the building collapsed. As the ceiling caved in and the walls buckled from the temblor, Emmanuel held his little daughter tight, perhaps knowing this would be the last thing he would do—he would save his little Alyanah.

The story is tragic, no question. But I can imagine the story Alyanah will be able to share with her friends and family as she grows older, the pride and awe she will feel as she remembers the father who gave his life to save hers. No doubt she will struggle with the loss. I know that feeling all too well. But I also imagine she will speak about her father with reverence. She will tell her friends about him. She will inspire others by sharing her story. And quite frankly, I wouldn't expect anything less. I hope little Alyanah will speak well of her father for the rest of her life. I hope she will tell the story and share the hope she found in her savior's sacrifice. It is a story well worth telling and a heroic feat worth honoring. And I have to smile as I think about the father's name, Emmanuel—"God with us" in Hebrew.

◙   ◙   ◙

What if someone gave his life for you? Would you consider altering your life out of respect and reverence? So why don't you?

For most of us, our lives are missing true authority. We live as if we're the ones calling the shots. We rely on our own strength, on our own talents, and on our own resolve. It's absurd, really. The Bible teaches that God has numbered our days, that he has given us life, that he gives us our talents, and that he oversees our comings and goings (Psalm 139). And yet we still try to handle life ourselves? Jesus himself reminds us that "without Me you can do nothing" (John 15:5, NKJV).

Let's not kid ourselves. It still takes faith to believe that the Bible is God's Word—and to submit to that authority.

I won't deny that. For many people, the need to surrender is a pretty big hang-up. Even for many Christians, it's hard to truly believe every promise found in the Bible and every teaching proclaimed by Jesus. But faith comes from hearing, and hearing by the word of Christ (Romans 10:17). So read his Word and your faith will grow strong!

But what if I told you that faith—real faith—is more reasonable than you think? What if I told you that, no matter how pragmatic and thorough you think you are, you practice just as much faith as any other person on a daily basis? You don't believe me?

"Faith is irrational, unreasonable, and downright irresponsible." That's what a skeptic will tell you. It's something I actually hear quite often. It is an argument against faith in general.

For the Christian, the argument takes on a much more subtle demeanor. Sure, we have faith. Sure, we believe in the Scriptures. But when it comes time to put it into practice, our true colors come out. Doubt sets in. Contingency plans unfold, just in case Jesus doesn't show up. It's our own form of unbelief . . . our own lack of faith in Jesus.

The fact is that we all practice faith on a daily basis. Grand faith, actually. Just not when it comes to Jesus.

Think about it.

Have you been to a restaurant lately? Who prepared your food? Did you meet the cooks? Were they trustworthy? How do you know? Did you do a background check? What would stop the chef or waiter—someone disgruntled with the world—from slipping something into your meal? You would never have known. By the time you found out, it would be too late. Maybe they had a death wish, and they wanted to take as many people as possible with them. You had no way of knowing. And yet you ate the meal without even thinking twice. You even enjoyed it! You trusted the restaurant and the cook! *Was that not faith?*

Several years ago, a few people poisoned the salad bar of a restaurant near my home. No one died, but many people got sick. The restaurant had to shut down for several days. But you know what? When the restaurant reopened, people returned. They kept eating from the salad bar. *Was that not faith?*

Have you been in for a checkup lately? How well do you know the doctor? Think about it—a complete stranger wearing a white lab coat. He or she could be totally untrained, for all you know. Maybe there was a medical degree on the wall. Did you see it? Did you read it? Could you tell me where your doctor went to medical school? How do you know that diploma wasn't generated on a home computer?

So what do you do for this stranger—the one with the poorly printed diploma on the wall? You take off your clothes. You sit in a thin cotton gown . . . forever . . . on a cold, hard table! You get poked and prodded. And once you've been completely humiliated, you receive a diagnosis and a treatment plan—scribbled illegibly on a piece of paper. Not only do you believe the diagnosis, *you follow the instructions to the letter*. What faith you have!

Let's take it one step further. You take the piece of paper from your doctor to another stranger in a white lab coat—a pharmacist—who is somehow able to read the illegible prescription (though you yourself have no clue what it says). After stepping away for several minutes, the pharmacist returns with a bottle of little white or pink or blue pills and tells you to take them. And what do you do? You take them! (How do you know this person wasn't the one who poisoned the salad bar?) You just exercised amazing faith, my friend!

I could go on and on, but I think you get the idea. The other day, I received my bank statement in the mail. It told me how much money I had in my account—represented by a number on a piece of paper. I believed I could go get that money if I wanted, but I didn't. Instead, I wrote a check for a plane ticket. I scribbled a few numbers on a check, signed my name, and gave it to the airline. *They took it!* In exchange, they gave me the opportunity to fly on one of their airplanes. It was piloted by a pilot and copilot I had never met. The flight crew served me food prepared by a chef I had never met. And I ate it. *That is faith!*

Come on now, let's get real. Our entire society operates on the basis of faith and trust. The airline took my check on faith. I boarded the plane in faith that the pilot was qualified to fly it. I had faith the food wasn't poisoned. And I had faith the airplane would get me where I needed to go in the time I needed to get there.

We all live by faith, but sometimes our faith can get us in trouble.

My son Andrew, his wife, Wendy, and their three kids were recently on a flight to Jamaica that overshot the runway. They were on their way to visit Wendy's parents (who are Jamaican), and the pilot was trying to land the plane in a blinding rainstorm at 11:00 at night. It skidded across the runway before breaking into three sections and coming to a stop just a few feet from the Caribbean Sea. Andrew and his family managed to escape by climbing out onto the wing, in the dark and the rain, and jumping a couple of feet down to the sand. (The jet engine had ripped away in the crash.) Smelling jet fuel, they ran down the beach for safety, only to be stopped by the rising tide. Barefoot, bruised, wet, and cold, they turned back and eventually reached a nearby road, where they were finally picked up by a passing bus and taken to safety.

Think of that. They, along with the other 140 passengers on board, nearly died. There they were, with three kids in tow, pushing debris aside, scrambling out of the exit door, finding their way in the darkness as the plane filled with smoke and fumes. Onto the wing, into the sand, barefoot, black-eyed from the collision, belongings destroyed. I'm amazed they made it out with so few injuries.

But before they got on the plane, how were they to know the pilot wouldn't be able to stop the plane in time? How were they to know they would end up only feet from the Caribbean Sea and barely escape with their lives? Do you think they would have gotten on that airplane if they had known what was coming—the rainstorm, the poor visibility, the pilot's inability to stop the airplane in time? No way! They had their children on board! But they had faith—in the airline, in the aircraft, and in the pilot. They also had faith in the Lord, of course, and he was the one who chose to spare their lives for his own glory.

We can't say that we don't practice faith. Faith is a part of our everyday lives. It's just that many of us don't like to practice faith when it comes to an invisible, apparently far-off God. But faith itself is a gift from God. The apostle Paul confirms this in his letter to the Ephesians: "For it is by grace you have been saved, through faith—and this not from yourselves, it is the gift of God" (Ephesians 2:8, NIV).

So, what's keeping you from putting your faith in God and having your life entirely transformed? Is it that you don't believe Jesus died for you, or do you believe but you just don't care? What's holding you back?

Do you truly believe that God can heal your marriage? Do you have faith that he can bring your wayward child back to you? Do you have faith that he can heal you from your pain? Or are those just empty beliefs? Faith is belief put into action. It must be exercised in order to grow.

◈　　◈　　◈

Growing up, my son Andrew struggled with the idea of faith and trust. He grew up in a great home. He had a superb father (if I do say so myself) and an amazing mother. As a family, we attended a great church, where Andrew didn't see much hypocrisy. He really had a good childhood, and he would tell you so himself. But even at the youngest of ages, he decided to go his own way. He turned his back on God. He drank. He partied. He did everything that parents wouldn't wish for their child. He's embarrassed to share some of the stories even today, and I don't want to hear them. They make him look so childish and self-involved. And, frankly, he was. But he and his friends thought they were great, invincible, and wonderful. They built their lives around themselves, around their parties, and around their fun—such great examples of individuals who believed fully in themselves.

Andrew carried on this way throughout high school and into college. He moved into a fraternity there and went even deeper into a destructive and self-involved lifestyle. Outside the constraints and support of home and family, he went downhill fast.

To Patricia's and my surprise (and relief), Andrew actually made it through college. (We were on our knees a lot.) He moved to Boston, slowed down his partying a little—mostly so he could make it to work in the mornings—and did his best to coast through life. Deep down, as he admits openly today, he knew he wasn't okay. He wore a great mask, but he knew his inner life was falling apart. He was becoming dependent on alcohol. He was losing friends left and right. And he knew that his prospects for the future were dimming. Just the other day, he shared with me a little perspective of that point in his life:

I thought I could defy the laws and boundaries of
life and yet be successful. But in reality, my life was
falling apart. The foundations I had built on were
crumbling, and things that had started as fun had
begun to enslave me, especially the alcohol. Partying
with my friends had started as fun. But here I was,
twenty-seven years old, and I was using alcohol for
different reasons. I was using it to cover the pain in
my life. I could never go to bed sober because lying
in bed at night, in the dark, my mind would race
and I would realize I was full of shame and guilt.
My only solution—the only one I was willing to
face—was drinking. If I couldn't find someone to
go out with, I would just drink by myself, watching
television until I fell asleep on the couch. That was
my life. That was my existence.

It was about that time—early February 1993—when my wife
and I tried one last-ditch effort to save our son from himself.
Knowing it was freezing cold in Boston, where he was living, I called him and invited him to one of our evangelistic
campaigns. As always, he politely declined—until he heard
it was in Jamaica. I knew he was thinking about sun, beer,
and the beach. And in his mind, he knew how to handle this
"religious thing." He agreed to come.

What Andrew wasn't expecting was that he would meet
a handful of young people his age who were living revolutionary lives. All had recently received Jesus Christ into

their hearts, and their lives had been radically changed. They had begun following Jesus and had amazing stories of God's power in their lives. Even more important, they were *enjoying* life far more than Andrew was.

"When I looked at their lives," he said, "I thought, *God, has this really been the answer the whole time? Can I really have a life like theirs if I just give my own life to you?*"

Heavy on Andrew's heart was the concept of eternity. (It's no surprise. It's on most people's minds if they ever take time to notice.) I remember his telling me, "If you had asked me earlier, I would have told you that eternity and the afterlife were unknowable. But in the dark . . . at night . . . when I was alone with my thoughts . . . I knew exactly what my situation was and I was so full of fear about eternity."

So he began calling out to God, while still in Jamaica, surrounded by others just like him. His simple prayer: "God, what is keeping me from you?"

In response to his prayer, God opened his eyes. He allowed Andrew to see everything that was keeping him from God. It was all the sinful garbage he had filled his life with. All the addiction, abuse, drugs—that was what was separating him from God. He was completely broken.

That night, Andrew committed his life to Jesus Christ. He asked God to forgive him of all his sin. He asked Jesus to make him new. And you know what? Jesus did.

For Andrew, it was a complete 180-degree turn. He left his old life in Boston and moved back to Portland, Oregon, to be close to family. He began working with me—sharing the Good News with others around the world. And he married Wendy—who was one of those amazing young people he had met that week in Jamaica. They now have three beautiful children, have been serving the Lord together for nearly twenty years, and have never looked back.

That is what a revolutionary faith does. It changes us in a thousand ways!

If you were to ask Andrew, he would simply say, "That is the way God does it. He takes something that is nothing—something that is completely broken—and makes it completely new." The old has gone. The new has come (2 Corinthians 5:17).

I can't help but imagine that there are many people who can relate to Andrew's story. You might be one of them. Maybe you've grown up with religion. You know what it teaches. You call yourself a Christian, but you still fight Christ's authority. It's a huge issue. And it's probably keeping you from a truly revolutionary life.

At some point, we all have to get serious about our faith. Christian and non-Christian alike, we have to stop and ask ourselves, what do I really believe about Jesus? Furthermore, am I living according to my beliefs on a daily basis? Is Jesus Christ "my Lord and my God," as the disciple Thomas so clearly states in John 20:28, or am I acting as if Jesus is just another religious leader among many?

You can handle a lot of life issues on your own. You can solve a lot of your own problems with personal resolve. But for real, powerful living, you need to *really* give your life over to the rightful authority—Jesus Christ, the Son of God.

◈   ◈   ◈

In case you've never had the chance to commit your life to Jesus Christ, I want to give you the opportunity right now. Even if you call yourself a Christian and know all the right answers, it doesn't mean you're actually living in accordance with God's will and purpose for your life. You have to fully trust him. You have to obey him. You have to surrender to Jesus Christ. "O my [child], give me your heart," the Lord calls. "May your eyes take delight in following my ways" (Proverbs 23:26).

If you have yet to even admit that Jesus is Lord, that's the first and most important issue you must resolve. You can take care of it today, right now. I don't want you to put it off.

I challenge you right now. If you have never asked Jesus Christ to be Lord of your life—to be your authority—do it right now. It doesn't take a special prayer or ritual. It's actually quite simple. And the facts are simple as well:

- God loved you so much that he sent his only Son, Jesus Christ, to save you. (John 3:16)
- Jesus Christ declared that he came that you might have life, and have it abundantly. (John 10:10)
- Jesus affirmed that he is the only way to God. (John 14:6)

- You know deep down that you fall short of the glory of God. (Romans 3:23)
- The reward for that shortcoming is death. (Romans 6:23)
- Yet while you were still a sinner, Jesus Christ died for you on the cross. (Romans 5:8)
- Jesus rose from the dead. (1 Corinthians 15:3-6)

Like I said, it's really quite simple. If you can't grasp it, go back and read the list again. With that knowledge, each person has a choice to make.

Who do you really believe that Jesus is? Are you living that reality today? Or, like Andrew was, are you living—in your own private way—in complete rebellion against God? It is up to each one of us to give in to God's authority, to hand our lives over to him, and then to watch him do powerful things through us.

11

A NEW KIND OF REBEL

I DIDN'T MEET Rosario Rivera the first night she came to see me. She didn't make it that far, and for that I am truly grateful. If we had met that evening in Lima, Peru, she's convinced she would have killed me.

Rosario was a young Marxist-Leninist fighter who had grown up in the slums of Lima. The injustice, pain, and suffering she had experienced as a young girl had left her bitter and angry. Born into poverty, Rosario had never finished her formal education. But she was a voracious reader. Her favorite authors, of course, were Marx and Lenin. By the age of thirteen, she was deeply engrossed in their writings. Captivated by the utopian society they envisioned, she believed every last bit of it.

By her eighteenth birthday, Rosario had bought completely into the Marxist cause. She traveled to Cuba, trained as a militant leader, and became a close follower of Che Guevara, the notorious Argentine Marxist revolutionary, taking orders directly from him. By her late twenties, Rosario was steeped in a lifestyle of death and bloodshed. She lived for it.

For years, Rosario followed after Guevara, fighting side by side with him, helping to further his cause throughout Latin America. Many times, she joined in the violence herself. Then, in 1967, she was sent on a surveillance mission to Bolivia. Guevara wanted to get a sense of the political climate; so naturally, he sent one of his most trusted followers.

Rosario's report, upon her return, wasn't optimistic. She warned Guevara not to go, feeling it wasn't the right time to enter Bolivia. In response, he spit in her face, kicked her out of his army, and went to Bolivia anyway, leaving Rosario in Peru. Within a matter of months, Guevara was captured and executed. Had Rosario stayed with him, she most likely would have suffered the same fate.

Rosario was crushed . . . and furious. She was still just as militant, just as angry, just as violent, and just as bitter as she had ever been. But now she lacked direction and leadership. She struggled for more than two years to find a cause to get behind—a vision to call her own. She still believed in the Marxist cause. She still wanted to see change. And as every day passed, she became more embittered and angry. That's when she heard I was coming to town.

In 1970, my team and I were invited to visit Peru to share in some regional evangelistic campaigns. When Rosario caught wind of our campaign, she was livid. She hated anything to do with God or Christianity, and the idea of a religious outreach taking place in *her* city set her teeth on edge. She was determined to disrupt the meetings in some way. If something worse were necessary, so be it. She was ready and waiting—and violence was not out of the question.

On the first night of our campaign, in a theater in the heart of the city, Rosario placed herself conspicuously among the crowd. She sat through the entire evening, her blood boiling with every minute that passed. My message that night was titled "Five Hells of Human Existence," in which I discussed the evils of murder, robbery, drugs and alcohol, hypocritical homes, and the real hell. As you can imagine, she hated me even more by the time I was finished.

When the invitation was given, Rosario decided to go forward with dozens of others. She wasn't thinking about praying with a counselor; she was thinking about murder—and I was in her sights. (Her plan was to case out the venue and then return the next night to do the deed.)

When Rosario reached the front of the theater, an elderly Peruvian woman, a volunteer counselor for the evening, approached her and asked, "My friend, can I help you receive Christ?" (That was why everyone else was coming forward.) Rosario instinctively turned and struck the woman. Then, noticing the commotion she had caused, Rosario ran out of the theater. (She told me later that if she'd had a gun that night, she would have killed me then and there.)

As she went home and went to bed, Rosario couldn't get the message from the evening out of her mind. She tossed and turned all night. She questioned her purpose, rethought her passions, and examined her way of life. Deep down, she knew she was wrong. She knew the message had the ring of truth. Finally, at five or so in the morning, Rosario fell to her knees by her cot in her room and prayed to receive Jesus Christ into her life.

Rosario herself told me that story years ago. It was rather surreal sitting across from a person who at one time had wanted so badly to kill me. But frankly, she was no longer the same person. She most definitely was still a revolutionary, but of a different sort. And personally, I'd say she's been a lot more effective as a Christian than she ever thought she was as a Marxist. She was truly, deeply, beautifully, and radically changed by faith in Jesus Christ.

Today, Rosario continues to work for social change, but not through the power of weapons, manipulation, or force. Now it's through the power of Jesus Christ and the Holy Spirit. She is relentless, yet so gentle, compared to her past. She is one of the most respected and trusted individuals in her community. She runs several ministries, offers practical help to hundreds of families, and serves thousands of young people. Her impact has been felt throughout the nation, and her story has been shared around the world. She still lives near the poor neighborhood where she was born, yet her heart for the people has revolutionized the area. Children are fed daily. Running water and electricity now serve the homes. Schools have been built. Churches have been planted. There is love, acceptance, and support. All thanks to her heroic efforts and her servant's heart.

"If my heart burned for the revolution in the past," Rosario once told me, "then it burns even more today. And if I did a lot for the poor before, then I do even more now." Above all, Rosario is convinced that only Jesus Christ can meet humanity's deepest needs. And she's found new purpose in her passion. Her life daily displays the virtues of the revolutionary faith the Lord Jesus Christ offers so powerfully.

◈   ◈   ◈

We all struggle with our purpose at times. We wonder why we're here, what difference we're making, and who really cares. It reminds me of my friend Raul. His dramatic story of change, similar to Rosario's, has challenged many. And it all started on a crowded sidewalk in the middle of a busy city.

Raul stood staring at a poster on the wall in front of him. It was a hot January afternoon, rather typical for San Jose, Costa Rica's capital city. As the day wound down, people from across the city made their way home for the evening. They were in a rush. Raul could hear the buses in the background, the people shouting from behind him. Life was busy, but Raul was not.

As the crowds around him hurried to get home, Raul

looked for an excuse to stay out. The last place he wanted to be was home.

Though only twenty-one years old, Raul felt much older. Life had been tough. His father drank heavily. His brothers were brutal bullies. His parents fought. And his community—for all intents and purposes—had turned its back on him and his family. To most, Raul and his clan were known simply as the poorest of the poor—the bottom of the barrel. And no one cared.

In that moment . . . on that sidewalk . . . in that city . . . Raul felt especially tired and very alone. But for some reason, he was drawn to one particular poster. The young man in the picture staring back at him was me.

For the past several years, Raul's home life had been in shambles. His family lived in the poorest area of the poor part of town. He and his brothers were infamous in the community, and his dad wasn't much better. As one of nine children, he was used to his parents' constant fighting. He learned to fend for himself and filled his days with whatever he felt like doing.

He and his brothers partied continuously. They drank, smoked, and did what they could to cause trouble. Deep down, he knew it all was pointless, but it was all he knew. "I was disoriented in everything," Raul told me years later. "My parents had a horrible relationship, and most would say my family had no future. . . . Then I saw that poster."

For some reason, standing on that street corner, he couldn't pull his eyes away from the advertisement.

The poster was for an initiative my team and I were putting on in San Jose. "Something in my heart told me I had to be there," he said. "For some reason, I felt God had put that advertisement there just for me."

He had no money for a bus, but he was determined to make it to the bullring, several miles away, where we were holding our event. Having never heard the Good News of Jesus Christ, he wasn't sure what to expect, but he was open.

"As I sat listening to the message," Raul recalled, "all I could think was, *Luis, someone told you about my life! Who told you? How do you know these things?*"

As soon as I gave an invitation for people to accept Jesus Christ, Raul confessed, "This Good News is for me!" That night, he committed his life to Jesus Christ.

Our initiative in San Jose lasted three weeks. Raul was there every night, soaking up the teaching. By the third day, he was singing in the choir. Raul was changed immediately. He quickly got involved in a church and was discipled personally by the pastor-leader. He started to learn more about the Bible. Even in those first days, he realized that God was calling him into full-time Christian work. He was determined to give his all to this new reality.

Doors began to open for him. He found a good job and began to work his way out of poverty. He started testifying about Jesus—in buses, in parks, wherever he was given the opportunity. By the age of twenty-four, he was coordinating nightly music and preaching events in an empty lot near his neighborhood.

Raul's family quickly followed in his faith. "Little by little, each one started to come to the Lord—all my siblings, cousins, aunts, and uncles. They started to see the change in my life and couldn't help but be affected."

Three years later, Raul started his first church and focused on discipleship and teaching. He worked diligently to raise up new believers in godly service. He went to university, furthered his education, and started a family.

Today, Raul is the senior pastor of one of the largest churches in San Jose, Costa Rica. On any given Sunday, more than ten thousand people flood through the doors of Iglesia Oasis de Esperanza to hear Raul preach his heart out. He is completely sold out for Jesus Christ and working just as diligently as the day he started. (And why shouldn't he? He preaches the same truth that radically changed his own life.)

The church has grown tremendously and gained respect throughout Costa Rica. In fact, this congregation—started by a poor nobody from the bad part of town—is now referred to by critics as the "rich man's church." Oh, how far they have come in just one generation.

Raul has started programs to teach and counsel other pastors in the area and has branched out to other countries, planting churches and encouraging individuals. His passion for the gospel of Jesus Christ has spilled over to his family as well. His wife and all three of his children (university-trained and bilingual) help to keep the church moving forward. In fact, his entire extended family now shares his faith in Jesus Christ—more than seventy people in all!

In the last few years, Raul and his team have helped to plant fifteen more churches throughout Costa Rica and beyond. They are working to spread the Good News in Chile, the Dominican Republic, Venezuela, Nicaragua, Mexico, and even the United States. Any resources they have go straight back to bless and encourage the local communities and meet the needs of the area, regardless of the recipients' faith.

Raul's impact has grown to reach tens of thousands. He has counseled doctors, lawyers, diplomats, and professionals throughout Costa Rica. He is not just a pastor, he is an ambassador—an ambassador for Jesus Christ. He is respected by everyone in the community and has shared the truth and reality of Jesus Christ in powerful ways.

Because of God's transforming work in Raul's life, Costa Rica will never be the same. Our world will never be the same. I truly believe that. And all this from a poor boy from a broken home, lost in a big city in a small nation in Central America.

That is what revolutionary faith in Jesus Christ can do.

◙   ◙   ◙

I can imagine what you're thinking: "That's great for Rosario and Raul, but I don't know them, I'll never meet them, and their experiences are different from mine."

In many ways, those two seem worlds away from you. In fact, their stories do seem extreme. But the reality of God's power to transform lives is available to us all—from the slums of Lima or San Jose to the mansions of South Florida. But it takes faith. It takes boldness. It takes passion. And most of all, it takes devotion to Jesus Christ. For "those who belong to Christ Jesus have nailed the passions and desires of their sinful nature to his cross and crucified them there" (Galatians 5:24).

Most revolutionaries throughout history have one thing in common—complete devotion to the cause. That makes people a little nervous these days. After all, the fanatics who hijacked those four flights on September 11, 2001, were devoted to a cause. And no one—I pray—wants to be like them. But where does that leave us? Apathetic and unwilling to fight—much less live—for a cause? For anyone to muster up enough conviction to make a difference—to have the strength and fortitude to see change—he or she must be committed to the cause.

In Mark 8:34, Jesus Christ says, "If any of you wants to be my follower, you must turn from your selfish ways, take up your cross, and follow me." He challenges us to bring glory to God, not to ourselves. But to bring glory to God, we must be committed to the cause. We must believe that Jesus is the Son of God, the chosen Messiah, who came to set us free from the bondage of sin and death. And quite frankly, if we do believe that, we really have no other option but to follow him.

I've been amazed by the number of Christians I have met over the years (mostly men) who wonder why their lives have gone south. Their wives no longer love them. Their children don't respect them. Their colleagues don't look up to them.

And they wonder why. After all, isn't that what we're taught in church? If you walk with God, you will be revered by men. If you trust God, you will find success.

In Henry David Thoreau's immortal words, "the mass of men lead lives of quiet desperation." Inevitably, it seems, men come to live apathetic lives. Sure, they believe in God. Of course they trust in Jesus and the promises he offers. But their passion is gone. Their excitement has faded, and everyone can tell. They have begun to let life live them as opposed to living life themselves, and they have no clue about their real purpose. But that doesn't have to be you.

Jesus came to give us "a rich and satisfying life" (John 10:10). He came to give us joy and to give us something to get excited about. He came to give us new purpose—and that is to bring glory to God. Do you believe that? Is that the life you are living today?

If you study the Scriptures for any length of time—especially the life of Jesus—you will most likely find at least one odd difference between his life and yours. Throughout his life, his ministry, and his teaching, Jesus was zealous for the respect and honor of God, not his own prestige. What set him off was not when someone slighted him or disrespected him, but when someone disrespected his Father in heaven. Just read about the time when Jesus cleansed the Temple (Mark 11:15-17; Luke 19:45-46). It wasn't because he wanted respect for himself. He knew he wouldn't get it, and he knew that wasn't his purpose.

He knew he had come to die—to give his life as a ransom

for us, who were lost and enslaved. And it was all worth it because he knew it would bring us—you and me—closer to God, just as it teaches in 1 Peter 3:18 (NIV): "For Christ died for sins once for all, the righteous for the unrighteous, to bring you to God."

I don't know about you, but I find myself revealing a different purpose on many occasions. I find myself fighting for my own honor—for my own respect, for my own glory—instead of God's. But where does that get me? Nowhere but frustrated, self-absorbed, and confused. I'd rather have God's purpose for my life than my own. I'd rather have his joy than some second-rate imitation in the guise of happiness. And there is only one way I can get it. To deny myself. To forget my agenda. To love God above all others. And to make it my life's purpose to point others to him.

As you focus on God, as you reorient your life toward him, you will discover a small but powerful secret. He will give the strength to sustain you. He will give you the fortitude to carry on. He will give you the power to persevere. You will be filled with God's Holy Spirit.

Don't forget who you are, and who God is in you. He is active. He is powerful. And you can "do everything through Christ, who gives [you] strength" (Philippians 4:13). We don't have the power in ourselves, but we have the power in Christ. And we have a new purpose in him. All he asks is that we offer what we have. We are to give him our resources, and he does the rest.

Only when we surrender, get on our knees, and get into

God's purposes will we be able to see true revolutionary change in our lives. Only after we stop pretending that we have all the answers and start living like Jesus will we ever see true, life-changing breakthrough.

Are you available? Available to God? Truly?

12

GOD'S AMBASSADOR

LIFE CAN SEEM rather easy when you have money. At least that's the lie we believe. And for someone with jets at his disposal, a world-class yacht at his beck and call, and more than enough resources to fulfill his every whim, it's hard not to give in to the lie.

My friend Wayne Huizenga Jr. knows that reality all too well.

Wayne is a strong, powerful, joyful man. I don't know if he has ever met anyone he doesn't like, and everyone seems to like him as well. He's the son of one of the most respected and successful CEOs in the world. Until recently, his father, Wayne Sr., owned the most exclusive golf resort in the United

States and one of the largest private yachts in the world. Wayne Jr. is a brilliant businessman in his own right and president of Huizenga Holdings, the group that helped start Blockbuster Video, AutoNation, and Waste Management (the largest waste disposal company in the United States). At one point, the Huizengas owned the Miami Dolphins, Florida Marlins, and Florida Panthers, and had ownership shares in several hotels throughout Florida.

I first met Wayne Jr. in 2003, during one of our evangelistic festivals in Fort Lauderdale. We were introduced by a mutual friend, and we immediately became friends.

As you can imagine, Wayne grew up in an interesting family—son to one of the most successful businessmen in North America. His world included private jets, European vacations, nice cars, big houses, great parties—the works. But you may be surprised to hear the story behind their success.

Starting out, Wayne's family was actually quite poor. Wayne Sr. started from scratch, barely scraping together enough money to buy an engagement ring for his girlfriend, and then borrowing money to buy a garbage truck after they were married. But as every great businessman does, he worked his way up, made some great deals, put in the long hours, and quickly made a name for himself—every ambitious man's dream.

Wayne Jr. knew that his father worked too much, but he couldn't help looking up to him. He had "the life." And no words of caution from his mother could keep him from pursuing the same lifestyle. As hard as she tried to keep Wayne

Jr. grounded, all he could do was watch his father and dream. No matter what his mom wanted for him, he wanted to be like his dad.

By the time Wayne graduated from college, his father was knee-deep in success from two historic ventures—Waste Management and Blockbuster Video. Wayne joined his father in the family business and began to help in the acquisition of other companies.

They got into the car business—buying out Alamo and National. They began AutoNation, now one of the largest new-car sellers in the United States. They started another waste disposal company (which has just recently become the largest of its kind in the nation). They got involved in the home security business. They bought sports teams. They traveled the world. They were making big money, and it seemed to come so easily. They had it all.

Wayne Jr. married a beautiful woman named Fonda and they started a family. He had the use of his dad's private jets and had a sport fishing boat he took all over the world. He had a huge house, nice cars, and hosted great parties. And if anyone had asked, he would have told them he was happy—very happy. After all, he had everything. Why wouldn't he be happy? But deep down, Wayne knew he partied too much. And he knew he wasn't all that a father should be. He tried, but never hard enough. And no matter the amount of success, true fulfillment never came. Deep down, he really wasn't very happy.

That's when Wayne met Brad, the captain of a nuclear

submarine. By a chance meeting, they became friends, spent three days on a sub together, and began sharing about life.

It didn't take long for Wayne to realize that Brad was different. He had a different perspective on the world. He had a different outlook on life. And for some reason, he seemed truly fulfilled. He had the "happy" that Wayne didn't.

Wayne finally got up enough courage to ask him, "Why are you so different?"

"Because I have Jesus Christ in my life," Brad responded. It left Wayne wondering, *Could it really be that easy? Could that really be it?*

Brad went on to explain to Wayne, "That's why you drink too much. That's why you're always out looking for that next big business deal. You're trying to fill a hole that *you* can't fill."

Wayne later explained to me and a few friends exactly what he was feeling: "It was as if my life was a never-ending Thanksgiving feast. I would eat . . . and eat . . . and indulge . . . and party . . . and never be full. It was painful. I knew Brad was right."

At that, Wayne finally got involved in a church. He assumed it was the next logical step, and for three years he sat in a pew and listened to sermons. But essentially his life wasn't much different. He still partied. He still looked to the world to fill the void. Only now, after the partying, he not only woke up with a hangover, his heart also ached.

It took three years for Wayne to finally realize that God wanted more than Sunday morning church attendance. God wanted Wayne to have a personal relationship with him, not just a relationship with the church. Finally, one Sunday night at church, in the middle of a booming thunderstorm, Wayne dropped to his knees—weeping—and fully committed his life to Jesus Christ. He realized he had finally played enough games. It was time to make Jesus Lord of his entire life.

Almost overnight, his life was transformed. He quit drinking, cold turkey. He stopped partying. He got more involved with his family. He became a better husband. (That took a little longer, but the process started right away.) He was more focused on his children. And he finally felt fulfilled. He had come to a point of true realization that no amount of success—no amount of worldly wealth—would satisfy the hunger in his soul. His perspective and focus had to be completely on God.

It turns out Brad was right.

Wayne is still a brilliant businessman. He didn't put his professional life on autopilot. His ventures have brought him and his family even greater success. But the business deals don't define him anymore. Material success doesn't drive him. Instead, he views everything he has and does as an opportunity to bring glory to God.

Now he lives to share the good news he found in Jesus Christ with the rest of the world. In fact, he and I often travel together to cities just to share his testimony. He doesn't get paid for it. He flies his own jet, at his own expense. He has no hidden agenda. He just found someone that changed his life . . . radically . . . and all he wants to do is share that truth with as many people as possible. It's a truth that has brought him far more joy and fulfillment than all the money in the world.

Shouldn't that be everyone's goal? How different would our lives be if we began living for God and not just for ourselves? What if our focus was to honor him—not ourselves—in everything we do? But how do we get there? Where does it start? How do we find true fulfillment and a right perspective? By realizing we are nothing more—and nothing less—than Christ's ambassadors.

In describing our ambassadorship, the apostle Paul says that it's "as though God were making his appeal through us. We implore [others] on Christ's behalf [to] be reconciled to God" (2 Corinthians 5:20, NIV).

That's no small matter. The implications are both powerful and liberating.

An ambassadorship, by any standard, is a privileged position. In the United States, the president handpicks these high-ranking officials and sends them out as his mouthpiece—his spokespeople. As such, it is the ambassadors' job to bring any message from their leader to the people of the land to which they've been sent. The message must be communicated officially, clearly, and well. An ambassador need not create the message, but rather simply deliver it.

Over the years, I have had the opportunity to meet with ambassadors in several nations, and I'm always impressed. They always carry themselves with dignity. They present themselves with confidence. They know their role and their responsibility—and the limits of their authority—and they take pride in their position.

As followers of Jesus Christ, we are called to be his ambassadors. We have been given a message and a mission, and we have been sent out to share it with the world. What an honor! What a challenge! But are we living up to it? Do we even know what the message is and to whom we've been sent?

For myself, I find great freedom and comfort in knowing that I am God's ambassador. Not only does it lend me dignity and power, it removes the burden of initiation. Ambassadors aren't in the business of creating their own message. In fact, if they do that, they will be fired. Their sole purpose is to listen to their leader and follow what he says.

So, as an ambassador of Christ, how are you doing?

◈　　◈　　◈

I was recently with Wayne Huizenga Jr. in Omaha, Nebraska. As he and I were sharing with a thousand top businessmen in the city, Wayne couldn't help but pull out his Bible and share a story. God had given him a message, and as a faithful ambassador, Wayne was compelled to share it. It was a story first told by Jesus himself, so it's well worth repeating.

There was a rich man who was dressed in purple and fine linen and lived in luxury every day. At his gate was laid a beggar named Lazarus, covered with sores and longing to eat what fell from the rich man's table. Even the dogs came and licked his sores.

The time came when the beggar died and the angels carried him to Abraham's side. The rich man also died and was buried. In hell, where he was in torment, he looked up and saw Abraham far away, with Lazarus by his side. So he called to him, "Father Abraham, have pity on me and send Lazarus to dip the tip of his finger in water and cool my tongue, because I am in agony in this fire."

But Abraham replied, "Son, remember that in your lifetime you received your good things, while Lazarus received bad things, but now he is comforted here and you are in agony. And besides all this, between us and you a great chasm has been fixed, so that those who want to go from here to you cannot, nor can anyone cross over from there to us."

He answered, "Then I beg you, father, send Lazarus to my father's house, for I have five brothers. Let him warn them, so that they will not also come to this place of torment."

Abraham replied, "They have Moses and the Prophets; let them listen to them."

"No, father Abraham," he said, "but if someone from the dead goes to them, they will repent."

He said to him, "If they do not listen to Moses and the Prophets, they will not be convinced even if someone rises from the dead." (Luke 16:19-31, NIV)

Think about that. The rich man thought he had fulfillment. He thought he had it all together, only to find too late that he had nothing. And there was nothing anyone could do to convince him otherwise.

We all have a date with destiny. The rich man and the poor man both died. Death is inevitable. But how we approach it—how we prepare for it—makes all the difference in the world. And there is no going back. Don't fall into the same predicament as the rich man. Don't forget your rightful place.

You have Moses and the prophets. You have the Bible. You have the truth. You know it. But are you willing to listen to it? And are you willing to share it? Just like the rich man, you may have a lot of things. But is that what defines you? Is that what you live for? Is that where you find your fulfillment? Or are you ready and waiting—listening to the Lord—for the assignment he has given you?

Whether you are an embittered, angry, socially conscious woman, like Rosario Rivera; a power-hungry, workaholic businessman, like Wayne Huizenga Jr.; or stuck somewhere in the middle, the message of Jesus Christ has the power to transform your life.

If you don't listen now, if you don't take it to heart today, when will you? It's one thing to call yourself a Christian. It's another thing to live like one—to live as an ambassador for Christ. And just like Wayne Jr. has told me several times, "It's easy to have a relationship with the church, but far more important to have a relationship with Jesus Christ."

Are you willing to be Christ's ambassador?

◧   ◧   ◧

Several years ago I was invited to the White House, along with several other religious leaders from around the nation, to meet with President Clinton. This was my first meeting with Mr. Clinton—whom I have since gotten to know a little better—and to say I wasn't a little nervous would be a lie.

During our time together, the president brought our small group into an intimate dining room for breakfast. He peppered us with questions, getting to know us on a more personal level. He asked questions about the spiritual climate of the nation and gained general insight into religious matters. As we continued with our breakfast, President Clinton slowly made his way around the room, asking questions of each individual based on his or her area of knowledge or expertise. I was naturally a little curious to see what direction he would take in his conversation with me. After finishing a brief discussion with another attendee, he turned to me and asked point-blank: "Luis, if someone were to ask you how late can you repent and have God still forgive you, how would you answer?"

The question caught me off guard, but by God's grace, an answer quickly popped into my head.

"Well, Mr. President, I would tell them the rabbi story."

I could tell I had his attention. He responded with interest, "What rabbi story?"

This is the story I told him:

A rabbi was teaching a class of Hebrew students
one morning when a pupil raised his hand and said,
"Rabbi, tell us, when should one repent of their
sins?" The rabbi stood up tall, stared the students in
the eye, and responded with complete confidence,
"Students, please pay close attention. Each person
should repent of their sins the day before they die."
At that, he sat down.

The students thought for a moment in silence.
Then a hand in the back rose up. "But, Rabbi," the
student said, "no one knows the exact day they will
die. How can we repent the day before we die?"

At that, the rabbi jumped to his feet and
challenged them, *"Then repent today!"*

When I finished the story, I looked back at the president.
With a slight smile and a nod he replied, "Good story. Good
story." That was it.

Each day, on average, 155,000 people die throughout the
world. Can you imagine? We don't know when our time will
be up. A friend of mine recently came home from a party,
didn't feel well, sat down, and was gone. Like that! Now, he
was ninety-one years old and had lived a good, long life, but
the suddenness of his death was no less shocking than if he
had been younger. And younger people die every day as well,
whether in a plane crash, car accident, or from illness.

It's a fact of life that people die. You could die. You *will*
die. Are you ready? Or are you just coasting along, looking

for fulfillment in other, less important things? Are you living out God's calling on your life? Are you fulfilling your role as his ambassador?

A very few people know when their day is coming—and usually that's because they're sick and the end is in view. For most of us, it catches us by surprise. Just when we least expect it. So, if you want to be ready, you have to prepare now. And quite frankly, the Bible and the redeeming power of the life, death, and resurrection of Jesus Christ are the only sufficient sources for preparedness. They have the power not only to prepare you for death, but to transform your life today—even to revolutionize it.

So why would you wait? Because you hate being confined to rules? Because you're uncomfortable with the message God has given you? That's all well and good, unless those rules are there to save your life, or the message is there to give you real fulfillment.

Do you already have the assurance of eternal life, or are you still on the way? You really shouldn't be wasting time. Settle this business right now. Why in the world would you wait? Jesus Christ emphatically states in John 10:28-29:

I give them eternal life, and they will never perish.
No one can snatch them away from me, for my
Father has given them to me, and he is more
powerful than anyone else. No one can snatch them
from the Father's hand.

Take time on your knees before the Lord and listen to his voice. Spend time in his Word—the Bible. What message is he giving you? What is he asking you to do? Are you ready to step up with dignity and power and live out that message?

13

GROUP THERAPY

JENNY'S LIFE WAS far from perfect. Although a successful manager at a busy coffee shop, she struggled with addiction, depression, and suicidal thoughts. Her family of origin had been a wreck, and despair had taken root in her heart. If you had met her at the time, she would have told you her life was miserable and she had little hope of change. Then one of her friends—another recovering addict in her Alcoholics Anonymous group—invited her to church. Like many, she was hesitant. She wasn't sure that religion was the answer to her problems. But she took a chance and showed up the following Sunday.

When Jenny arrived that sunny Sunday morning, parking

her car among the minivans and SUVs, nothing seemed too unusual. It was your regular suburban megachurch, meeting in an unassuming warehouse toward the back of a suburban office complex. Happy, smiling couples walked hand in hand toward the building, greeting neighbors as they approached the entrance. Nicely dressed children filed in behind their parents, with Bibles in tow. It seemed like business as usual. But for Jenny, there was something different about the church. As she sat through the service, she made mental note of it all. The music was different. The people were different. And the focus—according to Jenny—was far from what her critical heart had expected.

The focus was clearly on the person of Jesus. The Bible was clearly and plainly taught. And the people were loving, accepting, caring, and real—not perfect, but real.

By the end of the message, Jenny felt she had to talk with someone. She made her way to the front of the church, where she met the pastor and his wife. She shared her story, confessed her pain, and asked for prayer. She could tell they were people who cared—people she could trust.

The pastor and his wife did their best to comfort her and share the simple truth about Jesus Christ. And right then and there, in the midst of the noisy auditorium, Jenny asked Jesus Christ to come into her life and be her Lord.

The church leaders quickly took her under their wing and began teaching her more about the Bible. They connected her with a great family in the church who enfolded her into their circle of friends. Little by little, Jenny found a new way of living.

Of course, it hasn't all been easy for Jenny. She still has all her life issues to deal with. No question, there have been bumps in the road—setbacks, struggles, and quite a few terrifying moments. But when Jenny needs support, she knows where to turn. She knows where there are shoulders to cry on. She has a family she can trust.

Through the local church and the love of Jesus Christ, Jenny is now finding hope. Through the body of faithful believers, she has found a helping hand to pull her out of the ashes and to help her begin to write a new, beautiful story with her life. That is the work of the local church. That is the work of ambassadors for Christ.

◈　　◈　　◈

We all were born with a bent toward affiliation—a primal need for participation, community, and family. And it plays out in every aspect of our lives.

You were born into a family, surrounded by relatives. As a child, you took part in preschool or kindergarten, surrounded by other children. You continued on to grade school, middle school, and beyond, surrounded by other students. You joined Boy Scouts, or Girl Scouts, or some other social group. You participated on athletic teams. You joined the chess club, the science club, or the band. You looked for any sort of way to find others similar to you. It may have been subconscious. It may have been overt. But it's real. You crave affiliation.

Once you finally headed off on your own, what did you do? You went to college and lived in a dormitory with hundreds of other students. You moved to your own apartment, only to find roommates your same age and with similar interests. You looked for a spouse (or are looking right now). You started a family. You made friends. You joined an athletic club, a golf club, or a book club. You've lived your life surrounded by other people.

The desire to be part of a community is so ingrained in us that it even seeps into our technology. Some of the biggest, most successful companies today are based on what we now refer to as social media. They include companies such as Facebook, Twitter, MySpace, and LinkedIn—each one giving its own take on how we can stay connected as a community. And it's big business. (There are more than 400 million people actively using Facebook today!)

We are communal beings. We were designed for companionship. Even the greatest of introverts needs someone with whom to relate. It's why people get married and it's why they have friends. The local church is God's response to that innate desire in each of us. It keeps us connected to others. It keeps us grounded. It encourages us. Above all, it reminds us of our responsibilities.

But we all need a fresh perspective when it comes to the role of the church. As Christians, no matter our issues, our grudges, or our pains, we are the church and we are called to *act as* the church.

❖   ❖   ❖

One of the greatest gifts given to mankind is that of the church—the body of Christ. It is the only organization established by God. And though it is not perfect in its current state, it is powerful and beautiful.

Maybe you find that hard to believe right now. Maybe you've been burned by what you thought was the church, or maybe you're still struggling to find a community of believers in which you truly feel comfortable. If that's the case, I'm truly sorry, and I encourage you to keep looking. Why? Because the benefits—the pluses—far outweigh the negatives.

I'll defend the church to my dying day as one of the most inspiring, enticing, and enriching aspects of the Christian faith. For it is through the local church that we find true community, true relationships, true mentorship, and true accountability. Our fellow believers are the ones to whom we can run in times of trouble. They are the ones we know hold the same foundational truths close to their hearts. They are the ones we know are striving for the same purpose—the same goal. And as difficult as they may be at times, we know they have our best interests at heart.

For more than fifty years, I have been actively involved in a great church near Portland, Oregon. I'm not a pastor—that's not my calling. And though I serve on the board of elders, I seldom have the opportunity to truly help guide the church. Instead, I have the privilege of sitting under the teaching of others. I get the joy of true fellowship. I experience the reality of true community. And I get to be a part of God's greater family. I wouldn't change it for anything.

Too often—whether on the mission field or when I've been away on long campaigns—I have been separated from my church community. And having seen and felt the difference, I believe that nothing can replace the power of the church.

It was the local church that made it possible for Patricia and me to first go to the mission field. It was the local church who supported us while Patricia struggled with cancer. It was the local church who faithfully prayed for my son Andrew while he ran from God. Why would I not want that for someone else? Why would I not wish that for even my worst enemy?

The Bible reminds us—it even commands us—to be part of a local community of believers (Hebrews 10:25). Jesus exemplified it for us, taking every opportunity to meet with other believers and share God's Word.

It is only within the local church, the community of believers, that we can motivate one another to acts of love and good works. And that is why we are challenged to continue meeting together and to continue encouraging one another, even when others neglect to (Hebrews 10:24-25). In fact, in the Gospel of Matthew, Jesus himself reminds us of the importance of the church: "I will build my church, and all the powers of hell will not conquer it" (Matthew 16:18). That sounds serious. That sounds powerful.

In the book of Acts, the apostle Paul reminds us to look out for the church: "Guard yourselves and God's people. Feed and shepherd God's flock—his church, purchased with his own blood" (Acts 20:28).

It was through the local church that Wayne Huizenga Jr. found Jesus Christ and true fulfillment. It was through the local church that my friend Dave Hall found salvation. It was the local church who led my father to faith in Jesus Christ. It was the local church who trained up Raul, mentored Ingrid, and encouraged Rosario. It was the local church who supported Patricia and me during some of the most difficult times of our lives. And we all have the opportunity to be a part of that powerful force.

If you are reading these stories of radical change and wondering how your life can be like theirs, you must recognize the role the local church plays in the equation. It was essential to their growth and their foundation. Is it essential in your life as well?

In the community and activities of the local church, we can really grow. In the church, we can "be happy with those who are happy, and weep with those who weep" (Romans 12:15). But what are the marks of a solid church community? How do we know when we've found the real deal?

Reading through the Bible, we find many key factors that relate to the marks of a solid community of believers. Here are a few key factors to consider.

- Is Jesus Christ the center? All worship, singing, praying, financial contributions, and teaching should be about him—our Lord, Savior, and King.
- Is the Bible clearly taught, read, and obeyed? Is it treated as the Holy Scripture?
- Are people really loving one another? Does it show? Are they living out Christ's teaching in John 13:34: "Just as I have loved you, you should love each other"?

If you've already found a church that meets these criteria, praise the Lord. Make sure you get—and stay—plugged in. (You can't just get your feet wet. You've got to dive in head-first.) And thank the Lord for the blessing he has given you. If you haven't yet found a church that meets these key criteria—keep looking. Keep the faith. Ask the Lord to guide you. And don't give up. God wants you in a community of believers, and he doesn't want you to lower your standards. He wants you challenged, encouraged, and blessed by others on a daily basis. He wants you rejoicing with those who rejoice and mourning with those who mourn. And he wants you using your gifts to encourage and bless others.

God will point you in the right direction if you ask him. Granted, you won't ever find the *perfect* church, because the church is people and people aren't perfect. So don't set your standards ridiculously high. Don't expect an impossible perfection. You will find issues. You may be disappointed. But if you find a church that meets the three basic criteria—or if you're a part of one now—jump in, stop complaining, and start serving the Lord in that place. As you seek to be a blessing to others, you yourself will be blessed.

Many people criticize the church. But I wonder what Jenny would say. I wonder what her perspective would be after all the church has done for her. For me, I know the church is flawed. After all, it's full of sinners like me. Redeemed, yes, but still flawed. But the beauty it offers—the encouragement and blessing it brings—is worth it all by far.

14

MORE THAN KNOWING

IF YOU DON'T believe me by now, I'm not sure you will ever be convinced. God is ready and waiting to transform our broken and hurting world. He is ready and waiting to transform you and your situation.

The Good News made possible through Jesus Christ and preached by his followers is not just one of comfort, but also one of power. It affects economies, health care, social justice, morality, dignity, relationships, *and your stressful, tiring, everyday life.*

He offers you a guidebook for living.
He fills you with his knowledge and power.

He frees you from guilt and pain.
He establishes true authority.
He gives you new purpose.
He offers absolute assurance.
He surrounds you with a caring family.
And he lifts you up from the struggles of this life.

But you have to believe it with your whole heart, and you have to act on it. "For I am not ashamed of this Good News about Christ," the apostle Paul tells us in Romans 1:16. "It is the power of God at work, saving everyone who believes."

Many years ago, a weekly magazine shared a story about a young student in the small village of Kalinovka, Russia. Especially gifted at memorization, the young lad had learned to recite large portions of Scripture taught to him by the local priest. The enticement? Small sticks of candy. Over the course of several months, the priest taught the boy all four Gospels (Matthew, Mark, Luke, and John), which the boy then recited from memory in church one Sunday.

The boy inevitably grew up, eventually left the church, and lost touch with the priest. Even into his seventies, the man was still known to recite Scripture, yet now only to serve his own purposes. For the prized pupil—the one who had memorized so much of the Bible—was Nikita Khrushchev, the former assistant to Joseph Stalin and once the premier of the Soviet Union; the one who oversaw thousands of unjust arrests and was closely connected to the infamous purges of the late 1930s.[13] When Khrushchev was the Soviet Party secretary, he once said, "We say the name of God, but that is only a habit. We are atheists."[14]

We all know that it doesn't help just to *know* Scripture. I will say it again—you have to fully *believe* it. And you have to *act* on it. In the words of Jesus, "If you love me, obey my commandments" (John 14:15). Obedience is faith in action.

John W. Alexander, former president of InterVarsity Christian Fellowship, once wrote, "There is little merit inherent in the mere process of memorizing Scripture. One could memorize voluminous portions and be an atheist. Satan memorized enough to use it to tempt Jesus."[15]

I don't think he could be more correct. After all, as it says in the book of James, "You say you have faith, for you believe that there is one God. Good for you! Even the demons believe this, and they tremble in terror" (James 2:19).

It's one thing to know the Bible. It's another to actually live it—to let it penetrate your mind, your soul, and your entire life. And that, my friend, is the first step to truly experiencing a revolutionary life right now. You must know your Bible! How else do you expect to know the mind of God?

Memorizing portions of the Bible is, and has been, a fabulous bonus in my life. But don't just stop there. Learn to *live* it.

◈   ◈   ◈

God is a God of salvation. Not just salvation for our souls— but for our entire lives. And our experience of that eternal reality can begin today. But how? Through Jesus Christ. Not only is he our strength, he is also our example.

These days, I know it's hard to fully understand who Jesus was and is. There are so many caricatures and images and ideas of him. Some are completely false and harmful. And most, if not all, fall short of his true nature.

To truly understand Jesus, we must really dig into the Holy Scriptures—the Bible. We must embrace the truth—and the hard realities—we find there. And we must come to terms with some revolutionary thoughts. Central to everything, we must come to grips with the Incarnation—God in the flesh. As the apostle John puts it, "The Word [Jesus] became flesh and made his dwelling among us" (John 1:14, NIV). Fully God. Fully man. That is Jesus. So what does that tell us about ourselves?

Though Jesus truly was God in flesh, the Bible teaches that he laid aside his divinity when he came to earth. Jesus arrived as a small, frail, dependent baby. He was born into humble means and grew up like any other boy of his time. Jesus—the creator of the world—humbled himself and chose to act in obedience to his created order. Jesus ate and slept and did everything we have to do in our everyday lives. And it doesn't end there.

Jesus "grew in wisdom and in stature and in favor with God and all the people" (Luke 2:52). Jesus grew. Jesus learned. Jesus obeyed. His coming of age was a process, just as it is for you and me. Jesus was tempted. *Jesus was human!*

That is different from what many of us tend to believe

about Jesus. He clearly was, and is, God. He is part of the Holy Trinity. He is divine. But we can't forget that he was also fully human. He set aside his divinity to show us something different, to guide us in the way we should live—in total dependence upon God, counting on God's promises. And the evidence is found throughout the Gospels.

Jesus struggled with the temptation to sin (Hebrews 4:15). He was enticed by the devil (Luke 4:2). He asked questions—many times (Mark 9:19). He prayed for strength (Luke 22:39-44). He became weary (John 4:6). He was even overwhelmed by grief at times (John 11:33). And perhaps most poignant of all, he felt betrayed and abandoned. As he hung on the cross, Jesus uttered the honest words so many of us have spoken at times: "My God, my God, why have you abandoned me?" (Mark 15:34). Yet he persisted. He continued on. He fought the good fight, and he had the ability to succeed. Not because he was God, but because—as man—he was filled with the Holy Spirit (Luke 4:1).

What does this mean for you and me as we struggle through life, as we fight the good fight, and as we wonder where God is in the midst of our pain? It means that we can experience the same success that Jesus did. It means we can take hold of the same power through the Holy Spirit. It is available to you and me.

When Jesus ascended into heaven, he left behind a "helper"—the Holy Spirit (John 14:26, NKJV). He left for us the same Spirit that gave him the ability to live the life he lived, to do the things he did, and to resist the things he resisted. You don't believe me? Read the book of Acts. It reads like a mirror image of the four Gospels: Jesus heals the sick; Peter heals the sick. Jesus casts out demons; Paul casts out demons. Jesus raises the dead; Peter raises the dead. Jesus cures the blind; John cures the blind. These men were not God, but they were filled with the Holy Spirit of God—the same Spirit that filled Jesus Christ. They were filled with his divine power that "has given us everything we need for living a godly life" (2 Peter 1:3).

Once your spirit is alive—once you're plugged in to the right source—that's when you see real change. That's when you really begin to live. That's when you have everything you need. And the results? Revolutionary. Truly transformational.

The second you believe in Christ and give your life fully to him, the Holy Spirit fills you. He gives you real love. He gives you dignity and honor. He gives you authority and power (2 Timothy 1:7). He allows you the ability to focus on God, to accept responsibility, to give up control, and to focus on others instead of yourself. None of that—no matter how hard you try—can be fully attained without the Holy Spirit. After all, you are now a child of God (John 1:12).

But it's your choice. You have the option. You must choose him and decide to live connected to him on a daily basis. That is real living! And what a difference the one and only Son of God makes. It *is* revolutionary.

In Hebrews 12:1-2, we are challenged with a beautiful yet demanding reality:

Therefore, since we are surrounded by such a huge crowd of witnesses to the life of faith, let us strip off every weight that slows us down, especially the sin that so easily trips us up. And let us run with endurance the race God has set before us. We do this by keeping our eyes on Jesus, the champion who initiates and perfects our faith. Because of the joy awaiting him, he endured the cross, disregarding its shame. Now he is seated in the place of honor beside God's throne.

And he waits for us there.

To live a life of joy, peace, and power, we must make a choice. We must run with endurance. We must rid our lives of the things that wear us down. And we must fix our eyes on Jesus, who died for you and me. It's not a matter of *if* we can live this way. When we put our trust in Jesus—when we give him our whole hearts—we *know* we can live this way. We *know* we have the Holy Spirit living within us. It's just a matter of trusting that a life fully surrendered to him is truly possible. It's a matter of believing God and his promises above all else. Granted, we will not be instantly perfect. Perfection in our lives is a process that won't be fully completed this side of heaven (1 John 3:2). But we will change; we will be radically transformed into the likeness of Jesus (Romans 8:29).

As small children, we all feared something. For many of us, it was fear of the dark or water or monsters under the bed. Whatever our fears, they were real and they were distressing.

As our parents tucked us into bed or stood with arms open wide in the pool, they comforted us with promises. They reminded us of the solid facts: "There is nothing to be afraid of. I will be here. I will catch you. I will watch out for you."

Nothing changed. Nothing was different. It still was dark. The water still was deep. The monsters—in our minds—were still under the bed. But we were left with a choice: Focus on Mom and Dad or focus on the dark. Focus on Mom and Dad or focus on the water. When we learned to trust, we were able to move ahead with confidence.

We know the promises of God. But will we trust them?

- "He will neither fail you nor abandon you." (Deuteronomy 31:6)
- "My God shall supply all your need." (Philippians 4:19, NKJV)
- "The Spirit who lives in you is greater than the spirit who lives in the world." (1 John 4:4)
- "God causes everything to work together for the good of those who love God." (Romans 8:28)

We are not told that life will be easy. In fact, when we are encouraged in Hebrews 12:1, "let us run with endurance the race God has set before us," the word used for *race* can also be translated as *agony*. Life can be tough, it's true. Our lives are often demanding and grueling. We need endurance—a steady determination—to keep us going, even when everything within us wants to quit. Because after all, as Paul writes, "It is no longer I who live, but Christ lives in me. So I live in this earthly body by trusting in the Son of God, who loved me and gave himself for me" (Galatians 2:20).

Never forget that you are special to God. He rescued you from evil, sin, addiction, and hopelessness. You were rescued not only from what you were (in behavior), but also from what you would become. And today, you stand as a testimony—a true representation of the power of God.

God wants to use you. He sees you as you sit in the ash heap of life. He wants to pull you out. He wants to seat you with princes; to give you dignity, power, and authority (1 Samuel 2:8). He wants to give you every good gift (James 1:17). But you've got to get in the race! And when you do, the promises that follow are amazing: freedom, fulfillment, forgiveness, redemption, and riches in heaven, just to name a few! He promises life, and life to the full (John 10:10). What more could you want?

God knows our fears as we lie awake at night. And he doesn't ignore them. He faces them head-on. Our only decision—what's left in our hands—is whether we want to believe him.

Revolutionary faith means trusting Jesus for everything and believing him in all circumstances. It's more than just knowing Scripture. It's actually believing it *and* living it! When you get to that point, your world will begin to change. I guarantee it. I've heard my friend the Reverend John Stott put conversion to Christ and surrender to him this way: "It is a moment of decision that leads to a lifetime of adjustments."

15

BUILDING A CITY

A UNIVERSITY PROFESSOR once challenged me, "Palau, how can you go to country after country, where people have so many economic and social problems, and preach about the resurrected Christ? Can't you do something more practical for them?"

I had heard the argument before, so my answer didn't take long to formulate. "There isn't a better way to help them," I told him. "The people of this world create the problems of this world. If we can lead them to Christ, we will create a climate for other positive, practical changes to take place."

The professor was right, of course, that we live in a world full of immense problems. A world weighed down by famine, poverty, injustice, oppression, and environmental disasters. But as Christians, we can help alleviate such misery.

We are called to serve as Jesus served, feeding the hungry, caring for the sick, breaking the chains of the oppressed— and leading people to receive the gift of life in Jesus Christ. Through his death and resurrection, Jesus is our hope that lives can change.

Conversion leads to the greatest social action. Period. As people's lives are changed, they are different in their families, in their jobs, and in society.

I learned this early in my ministry. In November 1965, I was doing a live call-in television program in a small studio in South America. The setting was spectacular—a sprawling capital city set amongst volcanoes and lush green mountains. I had just prayed with a woman to receive Jesus Christ as her Savior and was on to the next call. Thus, I was somewhat caught off guard when a high-pitched, squeaky voice requested an appointment the next morning at 9:30. It was an odd request, but I agreed.

The next morning, a small, angry woman walked through the gates of the studio property, followed closely by two huge bodyguards. She clearly was someone important, yet not someone I even remotely recognized. As she entered the office, her eyes traveled to every corner of the room. Finally convinced we had not set an ambush for her, she sat down.

"You pastors and priests," she began with a sneer. "You are a bunch of thieves and liars and crooks. All you want is to deceive people. All you want is money!"

She went on that way for more than twenty minutes, swearing all the while and smoking every last bit from a steady progression of cigarettes. She was a firecracker.

I prayed silently, *Lord, how shall I handle this?* Seemingly exhausted, she finally sat down and slumped in her chair, and I finally got a word in edgewise.

"Madam," I said, "is there anything I can do for you? How can I help you?"

She stared at me for an instant and then broke into uncontrollable sobs. My colleagues and I were confused. When she finally composed herself and could speak again, the edge was gone from her voice. "You know," she said, "in the thirty-eight years I have lived, you are the first person who has ever asked me if he could help me."

"What is your name?" I asked.

She was suddenly hard again. "Why do you want to know my name?"

"Well, you've said a lot of things here, and I don't even know you. I just want to know how to address you."

"My name is Maria Benitez-Perez," she said triumphantly. I recognized the name as that of a large family of wealth and influence in the nation. "I am the national secretary of the party in this country. I am a Marxist-Leninist, and I am a materialist and an atheist. I don't believe in God."

With that she lit another cigarette and took off on another breathless tirade against me, all preachers and priests, and the church.

"Why did you come here?" I broke in. "Just to insult me?"

For the next three hours, she told me her story.

Maria had left home and run away from a religious school as a rebellious teenager. Some Marxists had befriended her. She began to believe what they were teaching. She got engrossed in the lifestyle and eventually became a party leader.

We talked for hours. And every time we got onto the subject of God, she became enraged. But I could tell there was something eating her up inside. It finally came out.

"Supposing there is a God," she said, "which I know there isn't—but just supposing there is—do you think he would take a woman like me and forgive me?"

"Maria, don't worry about what I think," I said. "Look at what God thinks." I opened my Bible to Hebrews 10:17 and turned the book so she could see.

"I don't believe in the Bible . . ."

"But we're just supposing there's a God, right? That's what you said. If we're just supposing, look at what he says: 'I will never again remember their sins and lawless deeds.'"

She waited, as if there had to be more.

"But listen," she said, "I've done bad things."

I repeated the verse: "I will never again remember their sins and lawless deeds."

"But I haven't told you half my story. I've hurt people. I've done criminal things." (I could tell in her eyes that she indeed had done some very bad things.)

I repeated the verse again: "I will never again remember their sins and lawless deeds."

"But I've led student riots where people were killed."

"I will never again remember their sins and lawless deeds."

Seventeen times I responded to Maria's objections and confessions with that divine promise from God's Word. And finally, when she had nothing left to say, I asked her, "Would you like Christ to forgive all that you've told me about, and all the rest that I don't even know?"

She still was fighting. "He can't do it."

"You want to try it?"

"If God could change someone like me, it would be a miracle."

"You're right."

Maria stared at me for a long moment. Finally, on the edge of tears, she responded in a whisper, "All right."

I led her in a simple prayer, confessing her sins, repenting, asking forgiveness, and receiving Jesus Christ. At that, we parted ways.

When I saw Maria again the following January, I was not prepared for what I encountered. Her face was a mess of purple blotches and bruises. Several of her front teeth were missing. She was in bad shape. She told me what had happened.

"At a meeting of all the leaders from the party in the country, I stood up and told them, 'I no longer want to be in this party. There is a God and I know him now. I believe in God and in Jesus Christ. I am resigning today.'"

Naturally, they didn't like what she had to say. A few days later, four of Maria's former comrades attacked her and smashed her face against an electrical pole. For weeks she was forced to hide in basements of churches and homes of her new fellow believers in Jesus.

"There's going to be a revolution in June," she told me matter-of-factly. "We've had it planned for months."

It was to be a typical Latin American uprising: students and agitators causing a disturbance in the streets, luring out the army, which would then be attacked and over-thrown. The national chairman of the party would take over the country.

Maria remained on the run until June, when her party leaders finally tracked her down. She talked her four captors into retreating to her father's farm where they could rest.

On the morning of the revolution, the leader came to talk to Maria, his longtime friend. She could tell there was something different about him. "Maria, why did you become a Christian? I thought I knew you."

She proceeded to tell him about her conversation with me months before, about the Bible, and about the comfort and acceptance she had found.

Her friend slowly opened up to her. "You know," he said, "I've been listening to that Christian radio station. They almost have me believing there is a God!"

"There is!" she said. "And he wants a relationship with you! Please, why don't you get out of this business? Look at the lives we've ruined. Please, take this Bible and read it. Come back to my father's farm, and we can talk some more."

Later that morning, the disturbance that was supposed

to trigger a revolution fizzled into chaos. Why? Because the leaders of the revolt were off at a ranch reading about God.

Did Maria's conversion to Jesus Christ have an impact on society? You'd better believe it! Her changed life—her radical testimony and boldness—altered the course of an entire nation.

❖   ❖   ❖

My time with Maria was certainly one of the most bizarre encounters of my life, but one of many I know of in which evangelism—the message of Jesus Christ—proved to be the best form of social action.

To suggest that the good news found in the Bible makes no contribution to solving the world's problems ignores history. Slavery was abolished in Britain by a group of men who were converted to Christ in the mass evangelistic campaigns of John and Charles Wesley and George Whitefield. In South Africa, Billy Graham's racially integrated campaigns brought blacks and whites together in large public meetings for the first time in that nation's history.

In the first century, the gospel of Jesus bridged cultural barriers between men and women, Jews and Gentiles, slaves and free. It radically changed the fabric of society. It taught corrupt tax collectors to become charitable givers. It taught slave owners to be loving brothers. It taught overzealous religious fanatics to be grace-filled and loving.

Leo Tolstoy, the great Russian novelist and author of *War*

and Peace, put it this way: "For thirty-five years of my life I was . . . a nihilist—not a revolutionary socialist, but a man who believed in nothing. Five years ago, faith came to me . . . and my whole life underwent a sudden transformation. What I had once wished for I wished for no longer, and I began to desire what I had never desired before."[16]

Just imagine a city in which a million people underwent that sort of transformation. Where people began to look out for others, to serve the needy in powerful ways, and to think of themselves as lower than others. That city would be completely revolutionized. Lives would change. Families would change. Neighborhoods would change. Schools, businesses, and governments would change. It's what I call a quiet revolution. And it is very much possible.

◙　◙　◙

God is focused on more than just individuals. He cares about families, communities, cities, and nations. In fact, he is in the midst of building an entire Kingdom right before our very eyes. Don't get me wrong. It won't be perfected until Jesus Christ returns. I don't buy the idea that humanity can usher in God's Kingdom. But I do believe we can make a powerful difference while we're here. And not only that, we are called to make a difference. We are called to be the salt of the earth (Matthew 5:13), to shine a light in the darkness (Matthew 5:16).

All around the world, individuals are being transformed.

Churches are coming together. The Good News is being proclaimed. And communities are seeing the tangible, positive benefits of God's love expressed through word and deed. It's a fact, a reality, lived out and experienced on a daily basis. And God is using people just like you to make it all possible. I've seen it firsthand—in Korea, Guatemala, Arkansas, and Texas. It's happening in some of the most religious cities in the world, as well as in some of the most liberal. No one can argue against or challenge the gospel when it is lived out. It's simply life-changing.

Even right here in my hometown of Portland, Oregon, I have seen God do powerful things through the local churches. It all starts when believers get together, pray for their city, and begin to dream about ways to engage their neighbors. God commands us, in Jeremiah 29:7, to "work for the peace and prosperity of the city where I sent you."

There have been pockets of light in Portland for years. After all, it was at Reed College in Portland that Donald Miller and his friends perfected the evangelistic confession booth that Miller describes in *Blue Like Jazz*. It was in Portland that William P. Young crafted his best-selling book, *The Shack*. In fact, the Christian community in Portland has been making an impact for quite some time. But it wasn't until a group of Christians got together and challenged each other to get dirty, to go against the flow, and to encourage the Christian and secular community to rub shoulders that we actually began to see real change. After all, isn't that what salt does—gets involved; gets mixed in? The results have been both refreshing and challenging.

The movement in Portland has come to be known as Season of Service. Through this citywide effort, churches such as Imago Dei, led by Rick McKinley, SouthLake Foursquare, Solid Rock Fellowship, Horizon Community, and dozens of others have joined with my son Kevin and our team to lead the way on powerful initiatives to engage and serve the metropolitan area. Over the past several years, we have incorporated the work of six hundred churches, twenty-seven thousand volunteers, and dozens of local businesses. Using Jeremiah 29:7 as our guide, we've put our heads together to actively explore what it looks like to "work for the peace and prosperity of the city where [God] sent [us]." For the local church, it's simply sharing the love of Jesus Christ in both word and deed—breaking down racial, economic, and social barriers to serve and share with those around us. In a city like Portland, known for its liberal stance on nearly every topic, the impact has been powerful. It's dirty, for sure. It's convoluted, no question. And it's always changing and adapting. But just like salt, the local church is mixing with culture and activating change. It's doing exactly what Jesus called it to do, and it's beautiful.

This community-wide initiative has taken the city by storm. Focused on five main areas—homelessness, hunger and poverty, health and wellness, the public schools, and the environment—the church has begun to engage culture on a massive scale. And the impact has been felt throughout the region.

Churches are coming together to offer free medical service to families in need. They are partnering directly with the City of Portland to mentor homeless families and offer them support. Churches are "adopting" public schools, using their own resources to bring revitalization and excitement back to some of the area's most hard-hit places. And now, in a city where the Christian community has seldom had a place at the table, the churches are looked at as a viable, relevant resource—a powerful force for long-lasting change. They are being sought out by community leaders. They are being invited to offer their expertise on some of the region's biggest problems.

It has become clear—even to Portland's liberal community—that the church of Jesus Christ has something powerful to offer. And in the midst of it all, we are unashamedly sharing the love of Christ when the opportunities present themselves.

Over the past few years more than five hundred community service projects have been accomplished, five community coalitions have been formed, sixty-two public schools have been served, and thousands of individuals have received free medical care. Compassion clinics are being held on a regular basis throughout the area and at-risk youth are finding support and encouragement. And the church community isn't stopping there. Over the past two years, they've taken it a step further, raising tens of thousands of dollars to bolster city-run programs.

Even the sometimes antagonistic liberal media can't help but notice the work. *USA Today* described the Portland story as "chock full of stereotype-busting subplots. The most intriguing of all might be the way the Season of Service has thrust the area's evangelicals into partnership with [city leaders]."[17]

Season of Service has received acclaim from *Religion & Ethics NewsWeekly* on PBS. *Reader's Digest* listed it in its "Best of 2009" issue. And even Portland's local *Willamette Week* newspaper (known for its often critical view of the church community in Portland) couldn't help but recognize how the church community "has moved its unashamedly evangelical operations into the most secular of cities with nary a peep of protest."[18]

That is the loving, local church in action. That is just one of the many beautiful things it has to offer. And as a Christian, you play a vital role. If you have Christ in your heart, you are part of his assembly, his crowd, his church.

◈　　◈　　◈

There is no question that we live in a dark and hurting world. We see trials, misfortunes, pain, and agony on a regular basis. In such a world, people are looking for hope. They are looking for something worthy in which to place their trust.

The Bible teaches that we are to share with people the

hope of glory. In Matthew 5:14-16, God implores us to take a stand for our faith: "You are the light of the world—like a city on a hilltop that cannot be hidden. No one lights a lamp and then puts it under a basket. Instead, a lamp is placed on a stand, where it gives light to everyone in the house. In the same way, let your good deeds shine out for all to see, so that everyone will praise your heavenly Father."

For a lost and dying generation, we—the church—are the light of the world.

Think of that. You are the light of the world! What a powerful promise. We—you and I—hold the key to life, happiness, joy, love, forgiveness, and eternity with our Lord! For "God has chosen to make known . . . the glorious riches of this mystery, which is Christ in you, the hope of glory" (Colossians 1:27, NIV). Do you see yourself in that light? Do you realize what you really have to offer this hurting world? If so, what are you doing about it? What are you doing to let your light shine? What are you doing to be the salt of the earth? It doesn't take much—just simple obedience and faith.

I'll never forget my time in Buenos Aires in 2008. For nearly a week, I watched from my hotel room as a massive festival stage slowly rose above the street below. The venue, Avenida 9 de Julio, was one of the largest for a festival in the history of our team. It's the world's widest boulevard and runs through the center of the city. I tracked the progress and prayed for the events that would happen in the major metropolis, a city of more than thirteen million inhabitants and home to some of the most powerful people in Argentina and Latin America.

As the time for the festival drew closer, the buzz in the city grew, and unique evangelistic opportunities came with each passing day. For me, the festival was a dream fulfilled—the result of much prayer and years of hard work. But for the churches in the area, and for tens of thousands of believers, it was so much more. This was their chance to make a powerful statement before their friends, neighbors, families, and the city as a whole. It was their opportunity to share Jesus Christ on a regional scale, their opportunity to let their light shine before men.

Thousands of believers in Argentina prayed about and participated in this unique festival experience. God used them mightily. Through their partnership, the Lord brought more than nine hundred thousand people out in just two days to hear the Good News in person. He used the festival to reach millions more through radio, television, the Internet, and print. For thousands of Christians, this festival was their "stand"—their means of giving light to a dark world.

To see thousands of believers shining their light before men, to be a part of such an incredible move of God, is both humbling and inspiring. Christ in us, the hope of glory. What a promise! His Good News proclaimed through the church. What a privilege! So, what is God asking you to do? How is he asking you to shine your light?

You don't need to have an evangelistic festival come to your town—as powerful as they are. You don't need a Season of Service campaign to see a difference in your community—as energizing as they can be. All you need to do is make yourself available, ask the Lord to guide you, and realize that you truly do have something to offer this hurting world. Maybe it's words of encouragement to a friend. Maybe it's your time for a neighbor. Maybe it's the clear gospel of Jesus Christ shared with a hurting family member. Letting your light shine may involve something as small as a conversation. Your "stand" may present itself at a time of gathering with friends and family, or while participating in a church outreach.

What will you do today to let your light shine before men? Even the simplest deeds—the most humble of actions—can have an impact on your community, your city, your region, your country, and even your world. All Maria Benitez-Perez did was stand up and tell her friends what she believed. And that alone changed the course of history for one South American nation.

◈　　◈　　◈

Over the last several years, I have had the privilege of being part of some pretty amazing moves of God around the world. Powerful outreach opportunities similar to the one in Buenos Aires. Major community-service initiatives like the one in Portland. And each one can be brought back to one specific moment—a point at which one individual (or a group of individuals) gave his or her life fully over to Jesus Christ and began walking with a new purpose. Others soon followed suit, a vision was cast, and faith was given legs. From that point on, it became like a tidal wave—an uncontrollable force breaking light into some of the darkest corners of the world. But none of it would have happened without the simple gospel truth . . . and one person's obedience to the Lord's calling.

It all starts with a choice to follow Jesus Christ.

16

BACK TO
THE PROMISED LAND

ONE OF MY favorite accounts in the Bible is that of Ruth and
Naomi. It is a beautiful, irresistible, honest story of redemption, forgiveness, and restoration. A reminder that life is never
too difficult, it is never too late, and situations are never too
big to keep us from our Lord. For myself and perhaps many
others, the details of this account are strikingly similar to
those of our own lives. Names have been changed. Cities are
different. Even some of the details have been tweaked. But
as we read it, we can see ourselves. We recognize the struggle.
We can relate.

If you remember, this is how the story goes . . .

The year was somewhere around 1140 BC. The setting,

Judea (also known as the Promised Land). It was in the days when the judges ruled and freedom reigned for the Israelites. Life was good. But within a matter of a few short years, the picture turned bleak for many in the area. A famine struck the land, and soon families were starving, people were suffering, and fear was running high. The economy dropped out from under the people, and many were struggling just to provide for their families.

In the village of Bethlehem, a husband and wife—Elimelech and Naomi—and their two young boys sat in their small home, debating the situation and looking for a viable solution. Elimelech knew the situation was dire. Naomi agreed they had to do something in order to survive. Loans were coming due. Bills were piling up. And food was running short. But every solution seemed unacceptable. If they stayed, they would starve. If they left, they would face any number of dangers and uncertainties. And where would they go?

Their options were few and unappealing. Egypt, to the south—the place from which their ancestors had fled from captivity just a few generations ago. Or the unknown territories of the north—where giants and dangers were said to lurk. Or Moab, to the east—the one place God had told them not to go. In the end, they chose Moab, which seemed the least of three evils.

After arriving in Moab, Elimelech died, leaving Naomi alone in a foreign land to raise her two boys. When the boys were grown, they married Moabite women, further establishing their distance from God and once again breaking his rules. (The Lord had warned the Israelites not to interact with the people of Moab and not to intermarry.) Their fate continued to spiral out of control as the two sons succumbed to the same demise as their father, dying of unspecified causes and leaving their wives and mother to fend for themselves. If it wasn't bad enough that Naomi lived in a foreign land, now she was left alone, with two daughters-in-law to look after and guide.

And so the story becomes one of three suffering widows—Naomi, Ruth, and Orpah.

In her distress, Naomi finally came to her senses and realized her mistake. Hearing word that the famine had ended in Judea, and coming to terms with how far she had traveled away from her home and her God, Naomi prepared to make the long and arduous trek back to her homeland, along with her sons' widows. But the tension was overwhelming. They were now a mixed family of Jew and Moabites, pulled in two different directions. Either way they went, someone would be leaving her heritage—her old life. Should they go the way of the Lord, returning to Naomi's life under his protection, or should they continue in the way of the world, the comfortable lifestyle they had been living in Moab for so many years?

Finally, the decision was made. They would go to Judea. They would go to the Promised Land—together as one family—to a life directed by God. But it was not so simple.

Partway through the journey, Naomi turned to her daughters-in-law—the women she had come to love and rely upon. With tears in her eyes, she told them to return to Moab. She knew it was too much to ask of them to leave their old lives. It was too much to expect of them to join her in Judea.

"Go back!" she said. "Go back to your mothers' homes. And may the LORD reward you for your kindness to your husbands and to me. May the LORD bless you with the security of another marriage."

"No," they replied. "We want to go with you to your people."

But Naomi wouldn't have it. As she hugged and kissed them, she said, "Why should you go on with me? Can I still give birth to other sons who could grow up to be your husbands? No, my daughters, return to your parents' homes!"

Orpah apparently was convinced by Naomi's logic. She knew the journey would be difficult and the pull to return to Moab—to her old life—was strong. She couldn't deny it. She kissed Naomi and said her good-byes. But Ruth clung tightly to her mother-in-law.

Naomi did all she could, through her tears and sobbing, to convince young Ruth to follow Orpah back to Moab— back to a safe existence of support and provision from her Moabite relatives.

"Look," she said, "your sister-in-law has gone back to her people and to her gods. You should do the same."

Ruth could not be swayed. "Don't ask me to leave you and turn back. Don't ask me again! Wherever you go, I will go. Wherever you live, I will live. Your people will be my people, and your God will be my God."

At that, Naomi knew she had lost the battle. She couldn't argue with her any longer. Ruth was determined to join her in Judea. And deep down, Naomi was glad.

Upon their return to Bethlehem—to the city Naomi had left some ten years prior—life still was difficult. In those times, at that moment, it was less than ideal to be a widow. There was no one to protect you; no one to look out for you; and worst of all, no one to provide for you. Ruth quickly jumped into action. She found a field at the height of harvest and asked to work the land. Not as a harvester. Not even as a hired hand. But as a beggar—a scavenger willing to follow the workers and pick up their scraps. And it was there, in the midst of her sad state, that her redeemer found her. His name was Boaz.

Boaz, the landowner, took a liking to Ruth. He saw something different in her. He recognized her hard work, her genuine attitude, and her humble commitment to the Lord. He saw her loyalty and was drawn to her authenticity. (It didn't hurt that she clearly showed her intentions toward him as well.) Nonetheless, Boaz saw something special, something unique. And he saved Ruth from her dire state. Not only her, but Naomi, his relative, as well.

Both of these women—in one beautiful move of grace—found a new beginning. They found security, acceptance, compassion, and redemption. They were offered a new life. And why? Because they returned to the Promised Land. Because they recognized their mistakes, they came to terms with their missteps, and they had the humility to ask for help—for a second chance. They returned to God.

For Ruth, it was a new experience, a fresh understanding. She was new to this life of following after God. But she was committed. She was excited. And she was ready. She jumped in with both feet. She did what was required and expected, and she served with her whole heart. The result was a new marriage, a new life, a new love, and a new reality.

Blessings overflowed.

For Naomi, it was a return to the familiar . . . to the blessing she had once known . . . to the Lord from whom she had walked away. I can only imagine her return to Judea was bittersweet. She was familiar with the land. She was related to the people. But she had turned her back on them. She had left in search of a better life. And now, she was journeying back as a broken widow, a sad shell of her former self. In her brokenness, she found redemption. In her return, she found acceptance—not only by her relatives and friends, but by her Lord.

◆　◆　◆

It's no coincidence that, throughout history, God often used famine to bring people back to himself. He uses tough times to bring about renewal, humility, and restoration—to wake us up, shake us up, and bring us up. Oftentimes we must be broken before we are willing to change. And such was the case for Naomi and her family.

The story should be familiar to us all. We've seen it in our own lives, among our own family members, or among our friends. We drift from our "homeland"—from the place the Lord has put us—in search of security. We forget, ignore, or deny the basics of our faith. We are consumed by the desire to succeed. And we find ourselves lost, far from the Lord, and far from our true purpose. We all can find a little bit of ourselves in this story.

Maybe you're like Ruth, a "foreigner" who is new to this whole idea of God. You've committed your life to Jesus Christ. You've made your way into the "Promised Land" and have made your camp under the Lord's protection. But life still gets tough at times. The work is difficult. You get tired, even exhausted, and wonder if it's all worth it. Was this really what you signed up for? Is this really all there is? Where is the joy? Where is the peace? And where is the break?

You are reminded of your sin on a daily basis. Past failures are thrown in your face at every turn. Satan and his followers see it as their full-time job to distract you, confuse you, entice you, and challenge you.

Look to Ruth! Trust her reality to be your own. You have a landowner—the one who owns the cattle on a thousand hills—who has already bought you for a price. (He gave his only Son for you!) Don't forget it. Don't steer away from it. Learn from the lives of others and stay strong under his protection and leading. Lean into him, seek after him, and focus solely on him. Make your prayer similar to Ruth's: "Wherever you go, Lord, I will go. Wherever you live, Lord, I will live."

With Jesus Christ as your compass, you will never be sorry. With the Holy Spirit guiding you as you listen and obey, you will always be in his will.

Maybe you relate more to Naomi—or even to her husband, Elimelech. Both were followers of the one true God. But, if you remember, Naomi and Elimelech left the Promised Land when things began to get difficult. They turned from God and trusted their own wisdom when the situation got sticky. They knew they were going where they shouldn't. They knew they were disobeying God. But they did it anyway. After all, it made sense in their minds. It "felt right" at the time.

Does that sound familiar? Does it describe your past . . . or even your present? You knew you shouldn't have married that individual, but you did anyway. You knew you shouldn't have treated that person that way, but you did anyway. You knew you should have forgiven, but instead you held a grudge. You knew you should have stayed in the Word, but instead you walked away. You got tired, life got difficult, and you took things into your own hands. You got comfortable. It was wrong, and you know it. That's why the wisest king of all time, King Solomon, instructs us in his book of Proverbs, "Trust in the LORD with all your heart; do not depend on your own understanding. Seek his will in all you do, and he will show you which path to take" (Proverbs 3:5-6). Naomi and Elimelech should have followed that advice. Yet again, God is good and he turned the whole episode into a glorious triumphant outcome.

Like Naomi and Elimelech, we tend toward despair when

our lives take us down painful paths. We wake up one day and find ourselves in unfamiliar territory, far from God and completely on our own. And then we begin to wonder if it's too late to turn back.

Life can be difficult at times. It is a fact—a reality. In fact, the Bible tells us that we will have trouble in this world (John 16:33). But the Lord has promised to take the "ashes" of our lives and turn them into beauty. Naomi is a testament to that reality. So is Ruth.

God can, and will, take your tragedy and turn it into victory . . . if you let him. But you have to let him. Like Ruth and Naomi, you have to turn to him. You have to give it up to him. You have to trust him to do his miraculous work.

Do you have "ashes" you wish could be swept away? Do you still have areas in your life that you just can't figure out or get under control? Do you still wonder about your calling in life? My dad knew his calling. He knew who he was with no wavering of conviction. And it reflected in his life *and* his death.

I finally and deeply learned that same revolutionary faith at the age of twenty-six. But can you say the same thing? Do you truly know what your purpose is in life? Can you tell me why you are here on this earth? Or as you lie awake at night—worried about finances, children, life insurance, mortgage payments, and your marriage—do you wonder what this is all about, how it all will end, and whether it will all be worth it?

From your vantage point, do you see tragedy or victory? Do you see ashes or beauty?

◈　　◈　　◈

Your number one priority in life is to bring honor and glory to God. That alone should dictate how you live your life, how you treat others, how you love your children, and how you treat your spouse. It should dictate how you work, how you play, and how you love. Your relationship with God should have—and will have—a direct impact on your life. So how is it going?

In the last several chapters, I have shared with you my own struggles—the lessons I've learned as I've sought the Lord's guidance and strength in my own life, as I've sought a closer relationship with him. You have heard stories of individuals around the world who have experienced the same life-changing power. And you have been challenged by the reality of what God truly has to offer each and every one of us.

By now you realize that you—from the day you surrendered to Jesus Christ—have the Holy Spirit living in you. He gives you power to do what is right. It's exactly what our Lord Jesus promised.

But you have to take hold of that promise. You have to accept it for yourself—on a daily basis. You have to trust him for it.

God wants to heal you—spiritually, emotionally, and

physically. He wants to redeem you. He wants to fill you by his Holy Spirit with knowledge and power. He wants to free you from guilt and pain. He wants to establish true authority in your life. He wants to give you new purpose. He wants to offer you absolute assurance. He wants to surround you with a caring family. And he wants to lift you up from the struggles of life in this fallen and often messy world.

Quite plainly, the Lord wants to revolutionize your life. And the only thing standing in the way is *you*. You have to let him into your life. You have to let him direct your path. You have to lay aside your own agenda—your own vision for your life—and look to him for guidance and strength.

In a world where Christianity is looked upon as just one more pathway to God, you know the claims of Christ are different. He is unique. His message has the ability to change individuals, communities, cities, and nations. The Lord is the God of salvation—not only the eternal salvation for our souls, but also our entire lives. And you can experience that eternal reality today, right here and now!

God is a loving God. You know that full well. He is a grace-filled, pursuant God. But are you prepared to meet him, to experience him, and to see his miraculous work in your life? Is your heart in the right place? Are you willing to truly trust—to sacrifice—on a daily basis? Are you plugged in to the right source? Do you rely on his Word? Are you connected to his people? Are you trusting him for everything? Are you ready to lay down your life, your desires, and your fears in order to follow him, learn from him, worship him, and honor him?

I pray it is so. I pray for a newfound fear to take hold in your heart. Not a fear that leaves you paralyzed, but a fear that compels you to action. A fear of the Almighty. A fear of the Savior. A fear that transforms you and breaks you. A fear that lifts you up. I pray for a changed heart for you. I pray that God uses you to turn the world upside down . . . or right-side up. And I truly believe he will. He promises it in Ezekiel 36:25-29.

Lord, help each one of us to see your will. Help us to hear your voice. Help us to live in your strength. Give us your eyes. Show us your love. Open us up to your world so that we may bring *you* joy.

Lord, raise us from the ash heap and set us among princes—not for *our* glory, but for your glory alone. Help us to live revolutionary lives full of you and your strength in order to shine your light among the nations.

◙   ◙   ◙

Someday your story will end. Someday you will stand before God and give an account of your life. In the end, the only things that will remain are those you have done for eternity. The Lord is speaking to you today. Respond to him! Let God use you so that when you come to the end of the race you can truly say, "I have fought the good fight, I have finished the race, I have kept the faith. Now there is in store for me the crown of righteousness, which the Lord, the righteous Judge, will award to me on that day—and not only to me, but also to all who have longed for his appearing" (2 Timothy 4:7-8, NIV).

You do not have to wait for heaven to experience a great, revolutionary life. You don't have to question whether your life is truly honoring him or bringing him glory. You can know! You can have a revolutionary life—here and now—today. It is real. It is tangible. And it is spectacular. You just have to trust him for it—and obey him in it. Live by his Word, not your own. And expect big things.

Now, "Let us fix our eyes on Jesus, the author and perfecter of our faith, who for the joy set before him endured the cross, scorning its shame, and sat down at the right hand of the throne of God. Consider him . . . so that you will not grow weary" (Hebrews 12:2-3, NIV).

It all comes back to Jesus—the author and perfecter of our faith. He is our strength. He is our example. He is our sustaining power. And he is ready and waiting to do mighty things in you.

GETTING TO THE END
OF OURSELVES

It was 1960. Christmas break was just days away. I was bidding my time, doing my best to stay focused on school, knowing full well that my mind was headed in other directions. I was twenty-six years old, had just met a beautiful girl named Patricia, and was in the process of becoming an American citizen. Doors of opportunity were opening all around me, and I was growing by leaps and bounds. My future seemed wide open, and I was excited.

It was a Wednesday morning—chapel day—and though my mind was in other places and on other things, attendance was mandatory.

I slipped into the auditorium at the last possible second,

finding a seat near the back where the not-so-stellar students played chess and read books instead of listening to the speaker. I settled into my chair and began thinking of all I had planned for Christmas break. But when the speaker took the stage, his thick British accent and punchy, staccato delivery caught my attention. And when he pointed his finger, I noticed it was partially cut off. My interest was piqued.

The speaker was Major Ian Thomas, founder and general director of a ministry known as Torchbearers. I wasn't familiar with the man, but I definitely was intrigued. And though his message was short—no more than twenty minutes—I soaked up every word as if they were golden.

Major Thomas's theme that winter morning was based on Exodus 3—Moses and the burning bush. The essence of his message was simple but truly revolutionary to me at the time. It was a lesson that had taken Moses forty long years in the wilderness to figure out: *He was nothing and God was everything.* It was a lesson I, too, had to learn.

The message unfolded in beautiful fashion, and I'll never forget the major's tagline: "Any old bush will do, as long as God is in the bush."

"God was trying to tell Moses," Major Thomas explained, his half-cut-off finger wagging at the crowd, "that I don't need a pretty bush or an educated bush or an eloquent bush. Any old bush will do, as long as I am in the bush. If I am going to use you, I am going to use you. It will not be you doing something for me, but me doing something through you."

He went on to explain the scene: "The burning bush in

the desert was likely a dry bunch of ugly little sticks that had hardly developed, yet Moses had to take off his shoes. Why? Because this was holy ground. Why? Because God was in the bush!"

Sitting in that cold, musty auditorium, I realized I was that kind of bush: a worthless, useless bunch of dried-up old sticks. I could do nothing for God. All my reading and studying and asking questions and trying to model myself after others was worthless. Everything in my ministry was worthless—*unless God was in the bush*. Only he could make something happen. Only he could make it work.

Major Thomas went on to tell of many Christian workers who had failed at first because they thought they had something to offer God. He himself had once imagined that because he was an aggressive, winsome, evangelistic sort, God could use him. But God didn't use him until he came to the end of himself.

I sat with tears in my eyes, thinking, *That's exactly my situation. I am at the end of myself.*

When the major closed his message by quoting Galatians 2:20, it all came together for me: "My old self has been crucified with Christ. It is no longer I who live, but Christ lives in me. So I live in this earthly body by trusting in the Son of God, who loved me and gave himself for me."

I ran back to my room in tears, my plans for Christmas break long since gone from my mind. As I fell to my knees next to my bunk, I prayed in Spanish, "Lord, now I get it. I understand! I see the light at the end of the tunnel. The whole thing is not I, but Christ in me. It's not what I'm going to do for you, but rather what you are going to do through me."

I stayed on my knees until lunchtime, an hour and a half later, skipping my next class to stay in communion with the Lord. I realized the reason I hated myself inside was because I wrongly loved myself outside. I asked God's forgiveness for my pride in thinking I was a step above my countrymen because I had been well educated and was fluent in English; and because I had worked in a bank and spoken on the radio and in a tent and in churches; and because I got to come to the United States and mingle with pastors, seminary professors, and other Christian leaders. I had thought I was really something. But God wasn't in the bush. I hadn't given him a chance.

That day marked the intellectual turning point in my spiritual life. The practical working out of my discovery would be lengthy and painful, but at least the realization had come. It was exciting beyond words. I could relax and rest in Jesus. He was going to do the work through me. What peace there was in knowing I could quit struggling!

Many Christians believe that if they work hard enough and pray long enough, they'll be successful. That's the essence of legalism. As sincere as these people may be, if they are relying on themselves, they are heading for a terrible fall.

This was the case with Moses when he killed the Egyptian who had beaten a Hebrew slave. He was sincere in his intentions, but he was relying on his own power, the weapons of the flesh.

And this was my situation when I came to the United States to further my biblical studies. I had big dreams I wanted to see quickly accomplished. My impatience led me to rely on my own power, not on the Lord's.

Ever since that winter day at Multnomah School of the Bible (now Multnomah University), Galatians 2:20 has been a revolutionary verse in my life. I have learned that this is the very heart of Christian living—for the foundation of Christianity is the cross and resurrection of Jesus Christ. The astonishing fact is that Jesus lives within the believer, and the two become one in spirit. The apostle Paul described this as "the mystery that has been kept hidden for ages and generations, but is now disclosed to the saints. To them God has chosen to make known among the Gentiles the glorious riches of this mystery, which is Christ in you, the hope of glory" (Colossians 1:26-27, NIV).

Jesus foretold this relationship in his high priestly prayer in the upper room (see John 17). He prayed especially that unity among believers would be a picture of the unity between himself and God the Father. "I pray also . . . that all of them may be one, Father, just as you are in me and I am in you. May they also be in us so that the world may believe that you have sent me. I have given them the glory that you gave me, that they may be one as we are one: I in them and you in me" (John 17:20-23, NIV).

Many Christians miss out on the thrill of Christian living because they have not understood that Jesus Christ literally lives within them—a fact they could not change if they wanted to. Throughout my teens and early twenties, although I believed in Christ, I did not realize this truth. I struggled to obey Jesus. I tried to bear fruit to the glory of God. But I did not understand that I did not have to do it on my own.

◙   ◙   ◙

In describing how Christians are to live in Christ, Jesus used a vivid image. "I am the true vine, and my Father is the gardener," he said. "He cuts off every branch in me that bears no fruit, while every branch that does bear fruit he prunes so that it will be even more fruitful. You are already clean because of the word I have spoken to you. Remain in me, and I will remain in you. No branch can bear fruit by itself; it must remain in the vine. Neither can you bear fruit unless you remain in me" (John 15:1-4, NIV). To be in Christ is to obey him gladly and to acknowledge him as Lord. As a boy, I remember my pastor saying that we are to live in a state of "constant conscious communion." Christians must not take Jesus for granted, or our relationship with him will suffer— just as our marriages and friendships suffer when we take others for granted. We must truly be in touch with him, in loving and worshipful obedience. We must choose him. We must claim him.

No more apathy.

No more passionless existence.

Christ in us, the hope of glory.

Discussion Guide

Chapter 1—Expect More

1. What does it mean to be truly transformed by Christ? Share your reactions to the radical transformation that took place in Brandy's life after she gave her life to Jesus Christ.
2. How does one become a "comfortable Christian"? Discuss how that kind of life contrasts with the adventure of faith and trust we were meant to live.
3. Wherever we fall on the spectrum of faith, we all have moments of despair and bouts of apathy. Share a time when you were able to come out on the other side, recognizing that you were made for far more than this.
4. What areas of unbelief are you struggling with today? In what specific aspects can you pray for the strength to put all your faith in God?
5. Discuss the spiritual impact of living a "Sunday only" type of faith.

Chapter 2—Know Thyself

1. What does it mean to know yourself? In what ways has your self-awareness changed over time?
2. Why is it important to know your purpose and value? What do these terms mean to a Christian? What might they mean to an atheist?

3. What does it mean to say you believe in God, and what effect does that belief have on your everyday life? If you don't believe in God, what does that mean for you?
4. Give examples of ways in which our society has tried to customize and censor God, paying attention to the teachings we like and leaving aside everything else.
5. What is the "big picture" of your life? How can focusing on the big picture help you to weather the ups and downs of daily life? Explain your answer.

Chapter 3—Better by Far
1. What captures your attention about the way Luis's father spent his last moments on earth?
2. What is the key difference between the way a believer in Jesus Christ views death and the way the world views it?
3. Explain what the statement "The solution to death is life" means to you.
4. What can you do to make sure your life counts and to live it as best you can until you are called home?

Chapter 4—Happy and Blessed
1. What actions and attitudes are required to sustain a revolutionary faith like that of Luis's father? What is keeping you from living your life with true revolutionary faith today?
2. What kinds of changes might you need to make in order to keep God first in your life?
3. Share some areas in which you've felt called by Christ to step out in faith. What is the cost of redirecting your life toward Jesus?

Chapter 5—Monsters of Depravity
1. Before reading this chapter, did you think that humans were essentially good or innately depraved? Considering Luis's commentary on Jeremiah 17:9 and Romans 3:23, how has your answer changed?
2. What is at the heart of unresolved guilt? Is there a difference between guilt and shame? Explain your answer.

3. What is the difference between the way believers view their guilt and the way unbelievers might?
4. What are God's promises to those who are struggling under the weight of sin and guilt?
5. In what ways is Christ's divine capacity for forgiveness distinct from human forgiveness? How is forgiveness the ultimate freedom from guilt?

Chapter 6—Where Your Authority Truly Lies

1. Have you ever been challenged to defend the accuracy or authority of the Bible? How did you respond?
2. How would your approach to everyday challenges and struggles change if you viewed the Bible as the true guidebook for living? Explain.
3. Share an example of how your view of God's Word and your understanding of Scripture have had a direct impact on your life.
4. Recall the last time you delved into the Bible with enthusiasm and zeal. What can you do to continue to take joy in all that God's Word has to offer?

Chapter 7—Beauty from Ashes

1. Share your reaction to the incredible transformation that took place in Ingrid's life when she chose to put her faith in God's hands. What can you learn from her story?
2. What is your own faith story? How has a relationship with God transformed your life?
3. What difficult situation are you going through today that God might use for his glory? Is there anything keeping you from choosing to rise above the pain of those circumstances?

Chapter 8—What the Bible Says about You

1. What are some of God's instructions that you find most difficult to implement in your life? Why do you think that is? What might you do to embrace his guidance rather than refute or run from it?

2. What it does it mean that the Bible is God's personal love letter to you?

3. Why do you think God ingrained in each of us an innate desire to be accepted and loved by our fathers? What does this say about the relationship God desires to have with us?

4. How can you make your relationship with your heavenly Father more real? How can you move from simply *knowing* about God's love to actually enjoying it and experiencing it?

Chapter 9—The Image of God

1. How do you distinguish between body, soul, and spirit? What would life be like if your body and soul were the only parts of the equation?

2. "The human spirit is what separates us from the rest of creation. It is what makes us unique." Share some things that make you unique.

3. Use Luis's lightbulb analogy to explain why it is so important to fully rely on God as the source of our strength. What difference does it make whether we are "plugged in" or not?

Chapter 10—Emmanuel: God With Us

1. Why do you think we hesitate to give God full control of our lives, even when we know that he knows our problems better than we do?

2. What are some areas of your life that you are still trying to control? What can you do to hand those areas of life over to God, who knows exactly how to make things right?

3. "Faith is belief put into action. It must be exercised in order to grow." What are some ways to intentionally grow your faith?

4. Share your thoughts about why so many people call themselves Christians but still fight Christ's authority.

Chapter 11—A New Kind of Rebel

1. Compare Rosario's zeal when she was a revolutionary follower of Che Guevara with her complete devotion to Jesus Christ today. How has her sense of purpose changed?

2. Explain what a life of revolutionary faith might look like. What sort of impact would you have on those around you?

3. When people first accept Christ's transforming presence in their lives, they are often filled with an exhilarating passion to follow him. How can believers be sure that these spiritual highs do not fade away when the immediate emotions do? Use examples from Rosario's and Raul's stories to explain your answer.

4. Reflect on Mark 8:34. What today might be keeping you from truly living out God's purpose in your life rather than your own?

Chapter 12—God's Ambassador

1. What is an ambassador? What is the purpose of ambassadors, and what type of relationship do they have with their leaders?

2. What does it mean to be an ambassador for Jesus Christ? What message has he given you as one of his ambassadors?

3. List some of the things that give you the most fulfillment in life. Which of these are of eternal value?

4. Share what Jesus' words in John 10:28-29 mean to you. How does what the world has to offer compare with Jesus' promise of eternal life?

Chapter 13—Group Therapy

1. Why do you think God created humans to be so community oriented? Of the social groups you participate in, which provide you with the most love and acceptance?

2. Describe how your church community has influenced your life in the areas of spiritual growth, accountability, mentorship, and relationships. If you don't belong to a church, share your thoughts on the advantages a community of believers has on one's life.

3. What advice or guidance might you offer to someone who has been hurt or disappointed by the church?

4. What are the most important factors to consider when you are looking for a church? Why is it so important to have a clear understanding of what the church stands for?

Chapter 14—More than Knowing

1. What is the connection between faith and action? Keeping James 2:19 in mind, can we experience the transforming power of Christ in our lives with faith alone? Explain your answer.
2. What are some areas of your spiritual life where you know exactly what must be done but still struggle to live out your faith?
3. In the context of this chapter, what does the word *revolutionary* mean? How can you pursue a more revolutionary faith in God?
4. Hebrews 12:1-2 challenges us to run with endurance and rid our lives of the things that weigh us down. What burdens, fears, or insecurities are weighing you down today?

Chapter 15—Building a City

1. "Conversion leads to the greatest social action." What does this statement mean? Give examples from your own experience or from the stories Luis shares in this chapter to support your answer.
2. In your own words, explain the salt analogy Luis uses to describe the church's impact on society.
3. How do you see your church responding to God's call in Matthew 5:14-16 to be the light of the world? How might your city benefit from your church's involvement?

Chapter 16—Back to the Promised Land

1. What was Elimelech's fate when he disobeyed God and left the Promised Land?
2. For Ruth, what do you think was the hardest part about journeying on to Judea with Naomi? Why do you think she decided to leave her homeland?
3. How does the story of Naomi and Ruth illustrate Christ's promise to bring beauty from ashes?
4. What are some areas in your life that you just can't figure out or control? How can you pray for God to redeem you as he did Naomi and Ruth?
5. In what ways are you standing in the way of God's desire to revolutionize your life?

About the Authors

LUIS PALAU

For more than fifty years, Luis Palau has been a powerful spokesman for the relevance, reality, and significance of spirituality for individuals around the world. His work as a speaker, teacher, author, and spiritual leader has taken him to more than seventy nations, and his campaigns have allowed him to present a clear case for Christianity to more than one billion people worldwide through television, radio, print, and live events.

Luis is known as one of the world's leading advocates for Christianity—standing strong for issues of faith and the importance of a vibrant, healthy spiritual life according to the teachings of the Bible. He is well respected around the world, and especially in Latin America, where he has spent much of his career—including several years of service in Colombia, Mexico, Peru, and Guatemala. Luis is regarded by many as the most influential spiritual leader in the past forty years in Central and South America.

He is the author of more than forty books, host of three international daily radio programs, and head of the Luis Palau Evangelistic Association. He has dedicated his life and career to presenting the claims of Jesus Christ to as many people as possible.

JAY FORDICE

Jay Fordice is a writer and key team member for the Luis Palau Evangelistic Association. He has served on the Palau Association's development team since 2003, working on donor communication. For the past several years, Jay has also worked closely with Luis Palau on numerous articles and book projects.

Prior to joining the Palau Association, Jay worked as a communications director and short-term-team coordinator for HCJB World Radio in Quito, Ecuador.

Jay and his wife, Michele, live in Portland, Oregon, with their two sons, Carter and Elliot.

Notes

1   Mark 9:17, 22 (emphasis added)
2   Mark 9:23
3   Mark 9:24, NASB (emphasis added)
4   Frank Newport, "This Christmas, 78% of Americans Identify as Christian," December 24, 2009; http://www.gallup.com/poll/124793/this-christmas-78-americans-identify-christian.aspx.
5   Philippians 1:23, NIV
6   Jeffrey Meyers, *Somerset Maugham: A Life* (New York: Vintage, 2004), 347.
7   Jean-Paul Sartre, *Being and Nothingness* (Paris: Gallimard, 1943).
8   NIV, emphasis added
9   Corrie ten Boom, *Tramp for the Lord* (New York: Jove, 1978), 53.
10 G. K. Chesterton, *Orthodoxy* (New York: John Lane, 1909), 9.
11 Josh McDowell, *Evidence That Demands a Verdict*, vol. 1 (San Bernardino, CA: Here's Life, 1972, 1979), 40–48.
12 ESV
13 "Still Munching Candy," *Parade* (11 February 1962).
14 "Nikita Khrushchev: Time's Man of the Year," *Time* (6 January 1958); http://www.time.com/time/subscriber/personoftheyear/archive/stories/1957.html.
15 "Memorizing and Meditating on the Word of God: Introduction"; http://www.preceptaustin.org/Memorizing_His_Word.htm.
16 Leo Tolstoy, *My Religion*, trans. Huntington Smith (La Mesa, AZ: Scriptoria Books, 2009), xiii.
17 Tom Krattenmaker, "'Jesus' Favorite City,'" *USA Today* (20 July 2009); http://tomkrattenmaker.com/?p=252.
18 Aaron Mesh, "Undercover Jesus," *Willamette Week* (20 May 2009); http://wweek.com/editorial/3528/12567.

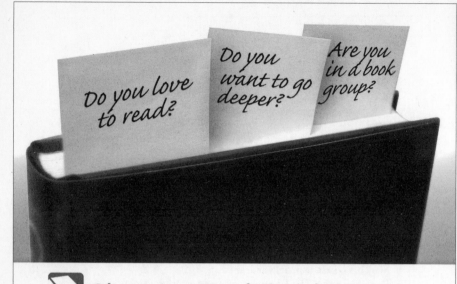